SUPPORTS

SUPPORTS:
An Alternative to Mass Housing

N. J. Habraken

Translated from the Dutch by
B. Valkenburg ARIBA

PRAEGER PUBLISHERS
New York · Washington

BOOKS THAT MATTER
Published in the United States of America in 1972 by Praeger Publishers,
Inc., 111 Fourth Avenue, New York, N.Y. 10003

This translation © 1972 in London, England, by Architectural Press

Library of Congress Catalog Card Number: 76-180866

Printed in Great Britain

CONTENTS

PREFACE to the
English language edition

This book was written because the existing man-made environment made no sense to the writer.

It was printed ten years ago. Four years later a group of Dutch architects provided the means and the moral support for research towards the realisation of support structures. Since then, the work done at SAR (Foundation for Architectural Research) has been based on the initial philosophy given in the following pages.

The world-wide interest in this work, together with numerous enquiries from foreign visitors, made me regret the fact that no adequate translation of the Dutch edition was available. An English edition, therefore, seems justified and may, I hope, contribute towards the universal search for a new strategy in housing.

Reading through the original edition again, I do not wish to alter anything I wrote. I feel, in fact, that it could have been written today. I have omitted one or two passages which were intended chiefly for Dutch readers, but this does not alter the fact that the entire book was a reaction to what was (and is) going on in Holland.

Now that so much work has been done on the actual design of support structures, the description of supports in the fourth chapter is more justified than ever, as what it was intended to be: a suggestion for *one* possibility among many. This description of a possible form was intended to provoke the reader into proffering his own suggestions for the design and construction of support structures. For this reason, no illustrations or drawings were given in the original edition; nor are they given here. I felt they would only subtract from the basic object of the argument: that the introduction of the dweller into the housing process should dictate decisions in design and organisation. Reader reaction has strengthened my conviction that variation in possible form and technique is apparently limitless and that design proposals can be judged only within a given social, economic and technical situation.

The idea of housing as a process in which every individual who needs a roof over his head has a role to play seems almost universally applicable, judging from the reaction outside the borders of this small country. But ideas, universal or not, can only bear fruit if they are cultivated in a given social environment. Readers tempted to do some cultivation themselves might be interested in our experience to date in this country. It seemed appropriate, therefore, to add a postscript giving some information on our pursuit of the support idea.

Eindhoven, August 1971.

INTRODUCTION

In the year 1918 a pamphlet was published in Rotterdam, containing barely fifty pages, which was entitled:
Standardisation in housing. A lecture by Dr H. P. Berlage.
With 30 illustrations and some suggestions by Ir J. van der Waerden.
Published on behalf of the Amsterdam Housing Congress of February 1918.
From this little book it appears that during the congress a speech was given by Mr van der Waerden in which he called for a number of quite drastic measures to combat the great post-war housing shortage. In the main, these measures concerned a thoroughgoing standardisation of plans and building elements, as well as the setting up of a central organisation for the distribution of building materials and labour. Apparently an exceedingly lively debate followed these suggestions, for Berlage later considered it advisable, in a talk to The Hague Society for Trade, Industry and Social Affairs, to explain why he had come out in favour of Van der Waerden's proposals.

Even to the reader who has only a superficial knowledge of the various controversies in the sphere of housing the texts of these two lectures, by the architect as well as the engineer, have a strangely familiar ring. On the one hand there is the technical expert, calling for the most rigorous standardisation and central control, because he sees in these the only solution, and on the other stands the form giver, who does not hesitate to call himself an artist, a man, moreover, who had already declared that *'to build is first and foremost to serve'* and therefore is principally concerned with the humanitarian side of the problem. He also recognises the need for the proposed measures. For it was evidently necessary to convince people of the value of these proposals in the light of the strong opposition to them which seems to have arisen. In his defence of the thesis Berlage wrote: 'I was stung by the great opposition to the advice, on the part of the workers as well as architects'.

1

I do not propose to pursue here the discussion which is hinted at in the pamphlet. What matters is that a remarkable conflict was generated concerning the housing of people. This conflict was born when proposals, put forward with the best intentions, met with opposition. Curiously, the opposition came from the very quarters in whose interest the proposals were made. Berlage himself summed up the character of the resistance: 'The workers—and this is the essence of the matter—see in the dreadful monotony of endless rows of identical houses and bungalows an assault upon their personality, upon their freedom, upon their humanity; this kind of housing turns one into a herd-animal, a serf, a dependent. And this is understandable. For after the long period of guardianship and distribution systems imposed on them from above, they fear that they will again be cut off from any say and initiative which they had slowly gained in the manner of their dwelling. And now this proposed form of housing, which has already been drastically characterised in a revolutionary organ as "one uniform, one fodder, one kennel", means to them being stacked away in some sort of cellular prison.'

So here we have a conflict between the method which from the professional point of view appears best, and the instinctive reaction against it on the part of the user.

This conflict forms the subject of the following pages.

For it is still with us. It concerns the way in which people shall be housed as much as the housing shortage which, in our day as in Berlage's, demands a solution.

Today a strictly uniform solution is still considered undesirable. Covering of a whole urban district according to a severely standardised system brings instinctive opposition, even though no one disputes the effectiveness of the system. The question hinges around the extent to which one can accept the full technical and economic implications of such a method.

But it is not my intention to participate, as the umpteenth contributor, in a discussion which has been around since 1918. Nor do I wish to take sides, either from the professional and technical standpoint, or from that of the users of whom Berlage spoke. My purpose lies elsewhere. I have wondered why this conflict has lasted so long! It would seem to be as tenacious as the housing shortage itself. And this observation suggests an important question:

Could the fact that a conflict exists between man and the method chosen to combat the half-century-old housing shortage mean that there is a connection between the two? Could it be that the housing shortage, or rather its apparent insolubility, is caused by the

2

antithesis between man and method?

This, in short, is the thesis I propose. An investigation into what is happening today shows that this antithesis has deeper roots than could have been suspected in 1918, and that its harmful effects can be seen in all aspects of modern housing. Not only can the shortcomings of housing, in human terms, be connected with it, but the whole building programme is being hampered by it to a large degree.

The method which has been referred to may be described as mass housing. The aspects of it which have aroused the resistance of the users are: the denial of involvement and initiative to the inhabitant. If it is proved from the investigation of the thesis here put forward that the housing shortage is indeed the result of the silent struggle between man and method, it will mean the condemnation of mass housing. It will mean that the mode of operation which has been followed until now has prevented us from providing the kind and quantity of housing we need.

The conclusion must be that the return of consultation and involvement on the part of the users, in the most literal sense, must be accepted.

Clearly, sound reasons are required to justify such a radical conclusion. Arguments arrived at merely from critical investigation, however acceptable they may seem, will therefore scarcely be sufficient. I feel that I can only venture to condemn mass housing because other solutions are possible. Criticism only makes sense if it contributes to something better. And I believe that this could indeed be the case. By accepting the involvement and initiative of the user as a starting point for contemporary housing, we may begin to see a way out of the constraints in which we operate. Unsuspected possibilities emerge. Both the technological and the human sides of the housing problem can acquire new perspectives. There is scarcely any limit to the possibilities which will be opened up, and new and long-lacking enrichment of life will again be within our grasp.

Housing is by no means an intractable problem. On the contrary: it looks as if a development is possible whereby the first steps towards a humane and modern way of housing could be taken. But in order to break through the barriers which stand in the way of a future development I mean to undertake a critical analysis of the present.

The following pages are the result of a preoccupation with future decisions, rather than those of yesterday or today.

3

PEOPLE

The housing process

Although everyone agrees that there is such a thing as a housing problem, it is not easy to put in a few words what the problem is. Is it simply an obstinate shortage of accommodation? Is it that there are too many complaints about quality and finish? Or does the impersonal character of the vast areas surrounding our cities give us a key to the problem? Can we learn from endless discussions going on about the living conditions of modern man and the way these shape people's lives? Has it to do with the questions which architects and town planners have to solve in fulfilling the tasks given to them? Or do the roots of the problem lie in the numerous attempts to provide dwellings according to the latest principles of prefabrication and factory production; attempts which refuse to succeed?

There are in fact plenty of problems in connexion with housing, but not one of these we can identify as *the housing problem*. This term, to be meaningful, must refer to housing as a whole, as a total concept. This is not the same as a large number of separate problems. Even the sum of all the difficulties mentioned above does not necessarily add up to a housing problem. We can only talk about a housing problem when all the difficulties connected with living and building slot together. That is when one problem causes another, or the solution of one problem depends on that of all the others.

Now this is indeed the case, and it could be underlined as follows. The engineer cannot hope for higher production without creating a swarm of problems of a non-technical nature which he, as engineer, cannot comprehend, let alone solve. The architect becomes more and more aware that in his design he cannot give a new impulse to housing because he conceives the dwelling as the result of technological and economic forces, and he can do little more than invent yet another variation on the theme given to him. If he tries to go beyond that, he steps outside his field, and encounters problems whose solution is not his business. The town planner may draw an ideal town, but knows that it could not be built because its realisation depends upon many other factors over which he has not, nor should have, any control. The inhabitant is aware that his personal wishes have no influence on what is happening because he is only asked to fill in questionnaires about dwelling requirements which deal with the provision of a dwelling in which he will never live. In short, those who are concerned with housing feel largely powerless to produce more and better results because action in their own field either appears to be insufficient or presupposes interrelated action on the part of many others. It looks as if the whole machinery for providing housing has seized up because the cog wheels do not mesh. But if this is so, we should not be examining some individual part of the whole, for in itself it is probably all right. The way in which it fits in with the others is what requires our attention. *There is a problem because the relationship of the various forces acting upon housing is in a state of crisis.* Like all fundamental problems the housing question is one of mutual relationships.

It is therefore necessary that we consider housing as a totality of events which cannot be looked at meaningfully in isolation from each other. We are dealing with mutually related forces arising from all sides of society and which, if all goes well, act in equilibrium. The action of these forces is the concept we call housing and the tangible results we call towns and dwellings.

I stress the widespread and comprehensive side, not in order to hide behind generalisations and commonplaces, but because only thus can we realise the impulses and influences which contribute to the creation of towns and the building of dwellings. The total shape of the housing process deserves our attention; indeed, as a creative event of the first order, it has gone too long without being properly understood.

The housing process is the common action of a society to fulfil certain conditions without which its existence would not be possible. This process is a fascinating phenomenon and it involves both rational considerations like construction, finance and organisation and impulses of a biological nature which are rooted in fundamental relationships of human existence.

It has never yet been investigated what laws it obeys or how precisely it functions. Yet it is this process which must occupy us, not the architectural problem or production or design questions. We know less about the forces resulting from the creation of cities and the housing of communities than we do about those which act upon the organisation of an ant heap. We do not even recognise the biological strategy underlying our building activity let alone control it or react to it.

It is true that in recent years several new factors have been introduced into the housing process, but these are little more than blind reactions to new technical possibilities. We should deceive ourselves in thinking that they are the result of the evolution of our way of life, which we understand mainly in terms of tradition and myth, and without knowledge beyond the technical and practical limits. It may be that the housing process has so far operated instinctively without raising any major objections but our society has reached a point where much that till now functioned as a matter of course has to be tackled consciously and rationally. As long as this is not done we should not be surprised to find that our housing is deficient, and we fail to solve one of our most fundamental problems.

A means of housing

One of the new factors recently introduced into the housing process is the system of mass housing. A quick glance in any direction will show that our society today employs this system for preference.

The provision of a large number of dwellings is seen as one project: similarly the design of a large number of dwellings becomes a single problem. It is an approach which at first sight seems the obvious solution. But its application has such far-reaching consequences that without close investigation we cannot form a clear picture of the nature of our housing, nor of the effect of our action in this field.

However, mass housing is generally considered merely as a method—which it sets out to be—and thus appears to be only a factor in the organisation and technique of housing. Its influence on other aspects is indeed recognised but its influence on the sum of these aspects, on the emerging process, is not seen. There is much confusion about this influence. Its true nature is hidden behind misconceptions and prejudice which makes any dialogue on housing a source of misunderstanding. It is therefore essential that it should be investigated more closely.

As has been said, the first point we notice about mass housing is its universal application, so universal indeed that housing generally and mass housing are regarded as almost synonymous concepts. If anyone, therefore, puts forward his notion

6

about housing it is automatically assumed that he is speaking about the way in which he wishes to apply mass housing. Any proposal for the solution of the housing problem is expected to mean yet another way of doing the same thing.

This is not an assumption we can permit ourselves, for mass housing is only one particular way to provide housing: dwelling and mass housing are related as end and means. When thinking about the housing process we may therefore regard MH (mass housing) as a means only, but not the sole and inevitable one. For if we consider MH and housing as synonymous we can only discuss the application of an *a priori* accepted technique. By being caught within the limitations of one aspect of housing we lose sight of the process in its entirety. If only to prevent this it becomes necessary to question MH as a means: not only whether it is the only means, but even whether it is the correct one.

Any particular method of providing dwellings is the result of the forces acting within the process, and may be seen more or less as the representation of technical and organisational factors. With MH this is indeed the case, only with one important proviso; namely the removal of one factor altogether. For MH is possible only if the individual inhabitant is not consulted about the manner in which his dwelling is realised. The influence which the individual, the layman, can bring to bear upon the process must be eliminated to make MH possible. The means of operation is therefore the result of a deliberate and clear interference with the forces acting on the housing process; a fact of the greatest importance for the form of our contemporary housing and our judgment on it. It cannot be denied that in thinking of the user we are dealing with an actual force in the total process, for if this were not so there would be no reason to fear his involvement as a disturbing and intractable influence. To those who cannot separate the notions of MH and housing the introduction of the user in the process is the beginning of chaos. It seems certain that to realise that this is not so would mean the end of MH.

MH as a work method is not new: the idea of building several dwellings as one project is quite ancient and was, I believe, well known to the Romans. But the situation in which we find ourselves is different because only now is MH seen as the *universal* way, and the fact is that in housing *the whole of society* the involvement of the individual is deemed to be undesirable. The general application of this method distinguishes us fundamentally from the way man has built earlier in history. It is not the fact that we have adopted new materials and technologies which separates us from our forefathers, but the simple decision regarding the position of the inhabitant. Our ideas of housing reduce him, in essence, to a statistic. Certainly it is hard to imagine how our society could have accomplished the genuine improvements in housing which have taken place over the last 50 years without the energetic application of MH. From this point of view the method, at least in the recent past, has proved effective. But because only now are we confronted with the notion of an entire society living in MH and because very few escape its implications, we begin to realise the contours of a process which reflects the negation of the individual. Therefore any inquiries into the usefulness of the method acquires a new and greater depth and reaches much further than measures concerning quality and quantity. Confronted with MH, we have to come to decisions regarding the total image of housing.

To this may be added that in a practical sense the effectiveness of MH can no longer be accepted without question, as is generally assumed. For new influences on the housing process have appeared which require a reorientation of method. For instance, it should be remembered that MH is usually justified because it is said to enable us to build many dwellings in a short time. And indeed more are being built than before its adoption. Nevertheless there are still too few dwellings. So if MH increases production, it does not increase it sufficiently for the needs of this operation. It is strange, in fact, that we are unable to produce enough, for production is, generally speaking, the least of our problems. The introduction of the machine has given us an industrial apparatus enabling us to produce so much that in many respects consumption becomes a greater problem than production. The conclusion to be drawn from this is that in effect there is as yet no industrialisation of housing. It is therefore a mistake to believe that MH and industrialisation go hand in hand. If that were so we should long since have overcome the housing shortage. After all, MH originated in the pre-industrial era, and it might just be that this method of increased production has become outdated by the coming of industrialisation. The rejection of MH, for whatever reason, does not necessarily mean a step back into the past. It will appear, as I hope to demonstrate, that the potential of industrialisation and standardisation will be realised only after abandoning MH and therefore through the reintroduction of the individual. But as has been said, one can only decide in these matters when the place and role of the individual, industry and MH have been defined in the play of forces

8

within the housing process.

No one has ever inquired what the presence or absence of the individual means. That he represents a force has only been recognised because MH has to oppose it. But what does that force consist of? How does it operate? How may it be applied? What influence does it exercise on other forces in the process? How can one establish a system of forces which will relate harmoniously to it? All these are absurd questions to those who confuse MH and housing, but to those who seriously wish to consider the housing question, who wish to test the functioning of the process, why it functions unsatisfactorily, and how it can be improved, they are questions of the utmost importance.

It is time, then, to break the bonds of MH, and at least to inquire what the individual can contribute to the housing process. Forces by themselves of course are neither destructive nor constructive: their effect lies in the direction in which they operate. If we consider housing as a task people will have to perform during their term in this world, it can be held that this task requires that the forces concerned in the provision of housing must be collected and directed by people blessed with intelligence. What is remarkable about MH is that the usefulness of the force we have referred to is denied *a priori*, and is therefore left outside the discussion. MH pretends that the involvement of the individual and all that it implies simply ought not to exist. The provision of housing therefore cannot be called a process of man housing himself. Man no longer houses himself: he is housed.

If we investigate the nature of the influence which the inhabitant can exercise it will soon appear that it is not negligible, for because it arises from the everyday actions of people it is closely connected with essential human activities. These activities of the individual turn out not to be the undesirable interference which MH has made them out to be, but are on the contrary so natural and self-evident, so simple and everyday, that it seems almost superfluous to mention them. At the same time they are so interwoven with human happiness and human dignity that they are far more than merely an influence in the housing process.

A dual requirement

In considering the role of the layman it is necessary at once to state that it is not in the first place his creature comforts which we are discussing.

It may be that the individual will be asked to make a certain

9

sacrifice to enable society as a whole to fulfil its housing task. It may also be that the immediate satisfaction of the dweller is not the main criterion because in one way or another the price society has to pay for this is too high. The desires and comforts of the individual, however important, as will presently appear, do not by themselves constitute a criterion. What matters is to what extent society can do without the involvement of the individual. Only when it is shown that this involvement is *essential* can we talk about an unacceptable limitation in our present situation.

That this is so will be seen when we consider certain of man's most essential requirements. It will then appear that only by means of active intervention on the part of the individual can certain requirements related to housing be satisfied. But—and this is most important—it further appears that the fulfilling of these requirements calls up those very forces whose absence in the housing process I have already referred to.

Let me explain this. When talking about man's requirements we might accept that MH as a work method would be effective if, in its ideal application, it provides the form of dwelling which fulfils all these requirements. And we are literally considering a form, a tangible structure, in which man is housed, and which assures for him the satisfaction of his requirements; for that is how the MH idea postulates it. The history of modern housing is therefore a search for ideal form. The greatest talents in the field of architecture and town planning have sought the liberating, all-providing design. Of course we need not criticise the fact that this ideal form has not yet been found, but the search is regrettable for other reasons. The ideal which has been pursued is not only unattainable because, like all ideals, it is subject to the imperfection of man's existence, but especially because the posing of the problem in itself excludes a solution. The brief of MH is paradoxical because a whole group of human requirements cannot be approached in this way. For is it not impossible to predetermine requirements which can only become apparent through the activity of the individual to be housed?

If this is accepted it follows that society cannot fulfil its task in the way it tries at present.

What then is the situation? The way in which MH approaches man's requirements assumes without question the possibility of translating these requirements into actual solid shapes, into architectural designs. These shapes can then be reproduced, and it is assumed that the success of the effort then lies in ever closer research into requirements, followed by an ever better solution in terms of form.

All this would be fine if it were indeed possible to deal with requirements in purely material terms. In fact this is only so in the case of requirements which today rate highly: consumer goods, where production is followed by consumption. But there are totally different requirements to be fulfilled in the field of housing; requirements which do not ask for products, but which are themselves productive or creative. If MH makes these activities impossible, does not that mean that a *complete* answer to the housing problem eludes us?

It is one of the wonders of our existence that the satisfaction of some requirements demands a very positive, personal, almost creative action on our part. Even today no one would maintain that we can live merely by consumption, no matter how attractively or skilfully consumer goods are presented. *But MH reduces the dwelling to a consumer article and the dweller to consumer.* For only in this way can it be expected that the consumer waits until he is offered a completed product.

It need not surprise us if this approach proves wrong because individual human action forms part of the housing brief. We are after all dealing with an important expression of human civilisation: to build dwellings is *par excellence* a civilised activity, and our civilisation is by no means confined to the activities of a number of more or less talented architects. That is perhaps the least part of it, for civilisation is first and foremost rooted in everyday actions of ordinary people going about their business. The material forms in which civilisation is expressed result in the first place from these simple daily tasks. But we are by now so accustomed to these forms that we tend to mistake them for civilisation itself. We imagine that, to produce, no matter how, or why, or by whom, means civilisation', whereas on the contrary civilisation is concerned with the interaction between people and their activities in terms of each other and their environment. When these activities result in tangible forms, these are symbols of a civilisation only by virtue of the manner in which they came about and which is reflected in their form.

When searching for the essence of an important aspect of our civilisation we should not only consider *what* is being done, but above all *who* does it, and why. In a sense it is, as will appear, much more important to understand how a dwelling comes about than what it looks like. MH takes away a man's act, and presents him with a form; it seeks to provide a comfortable form to be used by people who do not have to lift a finger to influence it. Does this not place MH, however skilful

11

it may be, beyond our civilisation? Following this line of thought, it is therefore justified to direct attention to the initiative and activities of the individual. In order to regain control over our housing we must rediscover what has been lost through a long preoccupation with MH, and regard it with a fresh eye.

The activity of the occupant

The activities which MH has rendered impossible are, to say it again, not of an architectural nature, for those we may safely leave to the professional. We are dealing with activities related to building and dwelling. It is about personal considerations and decisions, the formulating of one's own desires, and the coming to a judgment about a given work. It concerns the assessing and choosing of innumerable small details, the manifestation of preferences and whims. It concerns the freedom to know better than others, or to do the same as others. It has to do with the care to maintain, or the carelessness about private possessions, with the sudden urge to change as well as the stubborn desire to conserve and keep. It is related to the need to display and to create one's own environment, but also the desire to share that of others, or to follow a fashion. The need to give one's personal stamp is as important as the inclination to be unobtrusive. In short, it all has to do with the need for a personal environment where one can do as one likes; indeed it concerns one of the strongest urges of mankind: the desire for possession.

Now possession is different from property. We may possess something which is not our property, and conversely something may be our property which we do not possess. Property is a legal term, but the idea of possession is deeply rooted in us. In the light of our subject, it is therefore important to realise that possession is inextricably connected with action. To possess something we have to *take* possession. We have to make it part of ourselves, and it is therefore necessary to reach out for it. To possess something we have to take it in our hand, touch it, test it, put our stamp on it. Something becomes our possession because we make a sign on it, because we give it our name, or defile it, because it shows traces of our existence.

If, for instance, somebody borrows one of my books and smudges it, my annoyance would not be the same as it would be if the book did not belong to me. I am not annoyed because something has been damaged, for I too misuse my books, but because my possession has been interfered with. Only I have

12

the right to destroy what belongs to me!

We have the need to concern ourselves with that which touches us daily. Through this concern it begins to belong to us, and becomes a part of our lives. There is therefore nothing worse than to have to live among what is indifferent to our actions. We simply cannot get used to what appears intangible, to what receives no imprint from our hand. Above all we want to comprehend our environment. It is known that if this urge for possession has no other means of expression it would rather become destructive than look on passively. A child will destroy a toy with which he can do nothing, and content himself with playing with the pieces. A good educator therefore does not tell a child not to touch anything, but teaches it activities such as constructing, building, or maintenance and care. He gives a box of building blocks rather than a finished doll's house.

An invisible hand drives us to our environment without which we cannot experience our existence. If the contact which emerges from this is formless and irrational, we speak of barbarism; if it is ordered and sensible, we speak of civilisation. So what can we make of a manner of housing which denies this basic force, and in its intention is neither barbarism nor civilisation, but prefers a vacuum, a scientifically and organisationally justified *nothing* of material comfort which tries to satisfy the need for dwelling?

A means of self-expression

The inhabitants of a MH town cannot possess their town. They remain lodged in an environment which is no part of themselves. To identify with such an environment they will have to change; there is no other possible way. It is therefore said sometimes that the inhabitants 'are not yet ready for what is offered them', and that they 'have to grow into it'. Such an assertion is a complete reversal of the intention of all housing. It may occasionally be suitable in the case of a few minorities which are yet to be classified, but it has nothing to do with the normal town dweller with whom we are concerned. The question is not whether we have to adjust with difficulty to what has been produced with even more difficulty, but whether we make something which from the beginning is totally part of ourselves, for better or worse. Therefore what happens today is nothing but the production of perfected barracks. The tenement concept has been dragged out of the slums, provided with sanitation, air and light, and placed in the open. Important though it is that sanitation, light and air be available to all, the fact is that we only provided them in a gigantic barracks situation. The only way in which the population can make its impression on the immense armada of housing blocks which have got stranded around our city centres is to wear them out. Destruction is the only way left.

The initiatives I referred to have always come into operation when dwellers and dwelling found each other. The old houses left to us from the past bear witness to this. Each generation, each occupant, changed what he found. That is why in restorations more than one ceiling is found, or why panelling hides earlier, often more beautiful, wall decorations, why conservatories are added, doors blocked up and others formed, balconies removed or added, mullioned windows replaced by sash windows, window bars removed, gables replaced by cornices. These alterations were not always done for functional purposes. They were done to keep up with the times or because notions about living changed, because one could not identify with what one took over or because it belonged to a different generation. The occupant would rarely have been interested in aesthetic values, and anyway such considerations would change as much as the houses. But the house was an important means of illustrating his position in life. It was his social expression, his way of establishing his ego. For this it was necessary that the occupant should possess his dwelling in the fullest sense of the word. If changes were made it was not in order to preserve the building, but because one could not afford to pull down and start afresh. The occupant would not be interested in the original appearance of the house he now lived in. He only asked himself if the total corresponded with his idea of how a house ought to look, and if it did not, he would attempt to improve it. Only now are we concerned with the original appearance of houses, and we rebuild to restore. It is interesting to see how this urge to restoration increases in proportion to the decline of building as social activity. It would even be possible to interpret restoration of old buildings as a lack of self-confidence in our own building activity, and as a sign of the degeneration of building as a means of self-expression on the part of the user.

We cannot, moreover, draw the conclusion that the initiative to construct, improve or change is to be found only among the more affluent members of society. One has only to look at the backs of the poorer housing districts of some 40 years ago. The quantity of extensions, balconies, pigeon lofts, sheds, conservatories and roof houses come, in their chaotic character, as a relief to the observer who would rather see people than stones. They are the expressions, the primitive expressions, of the energy I spoke of.

Only few are able to occupy themselves with their possessions without affecting them. How many palaces and castles do we not find which bear the traces of a building urge for non-utilitarian motives. This building fever may far exceed the boundaries of reason. Old Europe is strewn with unfinished projects; works which outlived their initiators, or which had to be abandoned because the necessary means were exhausted. Building is an impulse which much prefers the act to the finished product. The wealthy patron, either as person or as institution, is a necessary phenomenon in society. But he is not the norm. The difference between him and the builder in the allotment is one of degree. Both decide, choose, test, make demands, and seek criteria, take initiative and perform actions. The one uses his hands, the other does not. What kings did, their subjects did also, only the kings' decisions were for architectural prestige, and this is preserved for posterity. But the history of building is quite a different story from the history of architecture. The latter concerns itself with forms, the former with a process, of actions taken which ultimately makes artistic endeavour possible. The creation of a building is sometimes an artistic event, but it is always an identification, and therefore it is of importance to us to note that this identification is closely connected with the urge to possess, which in MH is purposely frustrated.

The function of a dwelling

When the occupier is mentioned, as has just been done, we do not, of course, think only of the occupier as such, but also of that which is affected by his action. We therefore no longer talked about forces in the abstract, but rather about the interdependence between dweller and dwelling. In trying to understand the influence of the user on the housing process, this interdependence is of the utmost importance, for one can hardly think of dweller and dwelling as separate. The notion that they are strangers who come together more or less at random after the completion of the dwelling fits only the theory behind MH, but not reality. To see this we only have to ask what the idea 'dwelling' in fact means, and how it is used. Man himself, by his very presence, determines what a dwelling is. A dwelling is only a dwelling, *not* when it has a certain form, *not* when it fulfils certain conditions which have been written down after long study, *not* when certain dimensions and provisions have been made to comply with municipal by-laws, but only and exclusively when people come to live in it. The igloo is as much the dwelling of the Eskimo as the bamboo hut that of the Javanese. *The notion 'dwelling' is entirely subjective and is certainly not related to any particular form.*

The human act, in this case the act of dwelling, determines what a dwelling is. But this single truth is totally meaningless in MH, for to employ this method the tangible form of the dwelling must be known beforehand; it has to be determined unconditionally what the dwelling is which is to be produced in such large quantities. MH demands in advance what a dwelling is before the occupier is in any way concerned. Again it appears that the mass housing brief is a paradox. To avoid this dilemma MH accepts expressly that a dwelling is nothing but a particular object which can in itself be recognised as a dwelling. We might say that MH has discovered the dwelling as *thing* insofar as the existence of such a thing may be supposed.

But put like this, what is 'the dwelling'? It is a perplexing question if we are not allowed to answer that a dwelling is a place in which people live. What answer can we give then? If we build chicken coops, stables or barracks, and for lack of alternative people inhabit them, we have built dwellings. Any form I may propose and produce, for aesthetic, structural or moral reasons, becomes a dwelling the moment I can persuade people to live in them. *What is a dwelling?* This quasi-philosophical question is now being posed in all seriousness, and everything depends upon its answer. The demands which a dwelling has to satisfy are the basis of much serious research. Numerous forms are justified, numerous theories put forward, but who shall answer a question which is merely rhetorical? A question which has no answer, and which, were it not for MH, does not require answering?

If the housing issue were in a healthy state the need to question the nature and appearance of the dwelling would not arise: the contemporary dwelling would provide its own answer. But MH does not do that; in fact, by excluding the user from the equation it actually causes the question. One might even put it that not only does MH provide no answer, but it is in itself the question. That this is almost literally true will appear presently, when uniformity as characteristic of MH will be dealt with, for the moment a housing problem manifests itself, MH comes to the fore. This is the case now and in the past, but this does not mean that MH is a solution; it may be merely a symbol of the crisis situation.

Whatever the case may be, the fact is that in MH everyone is conditioned to the dwelling as 'thing', and to producing this 'thing'. All that is done, written or said, betrays this remarkable preoccupation. The simple assertion that the dwelling is the result of a process, and that it is this process which requires our attention in the first place, finds no hearing. Everyone wants to build dwellings, regardless of what is meant by the term; no one is prepared to regard housing in the light of a social activity preceding house building, especially insofar as this activity conditions the act of building. The search for the dwelling is in full spate, and follows a direction which is characteristic of the thought process underlying it. For the question is posed in terms of production: the problem is approached 'functionally'. The question: *what is a dwelling?* is replaced by the question: *what conditions are to be satisfied by the dwelling we want to make to fulfil its purpose?* We have already seen that the question in this form is deceptive because it is only concerned with a part of human housing needs. But the idea that these needs can be exclusively defined meets at present no opposition. On the contrary: it creates the impression that we are standing on firm ground and disturbing questions about 'the dwelling' are confined within a known scheme. A programme of requirements is set up and, after due study and interpretation, 'the dwelling' will emerge. There is much concern for the occupant: he is questioned and studied, lists of his needs and desires are drawn up; in short, he is treated as consumer of a product.

In harmony with all this we sometimes hear the remark that the dwelling is a 'machine for living'.* Not that anyone would seriously defend this notion, but the term is full of attractive associations of ideas because it creates the comforting impression that the dwelling poses no more complicated problems than the machine; in other words they are merely of a technical nature. There is no need to worry as long as our approach is functional. In its literal intention the slogan interprets the desire for MH, for only *if* the dwelling is a machine can it be designed according to a strictly impersonal definition of functions; the whole complicated relationship between dweller and dwelling can be, if not ignored, at least collectivised.

And yet no two things are further apart than the dwelling and the machine. For the purpose of the machine is to perform certain actions for us, while the dwelling should enable us to

*It was, I think, Le Corbusier who first spoke of a *'machine a habiter'*. Le Corbusier, as he repeatedly said himself, was *'un poete'*; his remark was meant purely poetically and forms part of his poetic sayings about the machine age, with the artist as its interpreter. It was functionalism which appropriated his metaphor, and turned it into a slogan, although Le Corbusier never was a functionalist!

perform certain actions ourselves. We live in it, a great part of our lives is 'performed' in it. If the dwelling has a function, it is that it exists to allow man to function, while the machine aims at the opposite. The machine does what we cannot or will not do, it performs actions which do not interest us as such, but which produce something we want. In this respect the machine is our materialised indifference: it is our stand-in in the production process and as such is the better the less we have to do with it. It presupposes our absence.

How then can the machine be compared with the dwelling which only becomes a dwelling by virtue of man's presence?

The natural relationship

I have tried to indicate how dwelling is first and foremost a relationship between people and environment, and because the relationship arises from the most common actions of daily life it is rooted in the foundations of our existence. I shall now attempt to show how this relationship can be an indispensable factor in the housing process.

A relationship relies upon actions, and dwelling is after all doing something; it is the sum of human actions within a certain framework, within the protective environment created by man. These human actions affect the environment itself. Because man wishes to possess his environment he takes hold of it. He decorates his walls, knocks nails in them, pushes chairs around, hangs curtains. Presently he does some carpentry, renews a floor, improves the heating, changes the lighting. From this point we can no longer draw a line which denotes the change to an activity we call building. Dwelling is indissolubly connected with building, with forming the protective environment. These two notions cannot be separated, but together comprise the notion man housing himself; dwelling *is* building. We are constantly faced with the results of the same relation between man and matter.

This relationship therefore is the basis for all that has to be done in the matter of human habitation. It is the outcome of human nature, and I will therefore call it the 'natural relationship'.

The natural relationship, thus defined, places us before the kernel of the housing process. From it spring the enormous activities, the specialisations of techniques and areas of knowledge, the thousand aspects of building and building organisation. It all started at a primitive stage when this relationship expressed itself directly in the action of man who by himself, without any help, built his protective environment. For although nowadays virtually everything necessary

18

for the creation of a protective environment can take place outside the immediate influence of the natural relationship, the latter remains nonetheless the criterion for all that happens.

I do not mean to say that we have to reject everything which is being done at present in the field of housing, but that room has to be found within the whole complex of activities for the natural relationship.

Man must relate to matter: a new order has to be created. That is why I spoke of a force in the play of forces of our way of housing, for the natural relationship is a central force round which the whole system moves. The natural relationship is a source of energy and of impulses. It is multi-sided, accidental, capricious and possibly elusive, but must try to hold the housing process in a firm grip, to give it direction, and constantly to feed it.

I propose to illustrate the influence of this force by indicating the evil results of its absence in all aspects of present-day housing. Briefly, today's situation burdens society in two ways. Firstly, in the absence of the contribution of the natural relationship, it has to be replaced by something else. MH requires builders to imagine what would happen if the natural relationship did in fact operate, and therefore places him before a chain of guesses. All impulsive variation, all everyday inventiveness, all spontaneity, the whole growth of testing and searching for more and better, which is what the natural relationship consists of, is now to be introduced, as it were, artificially, from outside.

But, secondly, it is not only necessary to substitute what has been lost in energy, but as much energy again is needed to prevent this guessing game being contaminated by the influence of the individual, for the interruption of the natural relationship does not mean that these forces are no longer present. The natural sources of energy cannot be checked. Great pains have to be taken to prevent the whims of daily life from interfering with the chosen method or preventing its effectiveness. To oppose people's idiosyncratic desires and maintain a reasonable collectivity more restrictions are necessary and greater friction is produced than can be guessed at. And I am not even speaking of the frustrations in human society which, as will appear, cannot be estimated.

It is evident that if in an equilibrium of forces one of these forces is neutralised, the mutual relations of the remaining forces will be disturbed. It may happen that a new equilibrium will be attained, but it may also be that this will not occur

19

because the remaining forces will predominate, so that the whole system begins to move in one direction, and drives towards an even more extreme situation. Something like this has happened with our housing. The tendencies we can observe in housing and house building are moving in only one direction. It need not surprise us if it appears that this direction points away from man and is drawing slowly but surely away from the human condition, like an ocean liner leaving a quay.

If all this happens in the simple relationship between man and dwelling, we shall find it multiplied a thousandfold in the relationship between society and the city; between men and dwellings, for the housing process has to be considered on that scale. Or rather we see the lack of the natural relationship immeasurably magnified in the town of today. This will become evident when we see the phenomenon of the present-day town in its true light; characterised by a want; a town where the natural relationship is absent.

CITIES

Uniformity as a symptom

It is well known that all the products of MH, without exception, have the appearance of uniformity. No other form of housing results in series of identical dwellings. In contrast to the general belief that this phenomenon has to do with factory production, it is in fact the direct result of the disruption of the natural relationship. The only way to ensure uniformity is the rigorous exclusion of the action of individual man. This rule holds good in the manufacture of pots and pans as well as in the formation of an army. As soon as the individual influences the process, nuances arise, and unwanted variations cannot be avoided. This is the charm of the hand-made object, and the bane of the sergeant-major whose duty it is to make sure that his troops are dressed uniformly and behave uniformly.

The results of the production line with which we have become so familiar make us accept as a matter of course that uniformity in objects is inescapable. The machine, that device which assumes the absence of man, overwhelms us with uniform products. That is why we must not misunderstand the reason for this uniformity, for it is not due to the action of the machine, but to the non-action of man. The machine is only a most effective means to avoid this action. We are too ready to blame the machine for all this uniformity—which in other cases is justified. But it is a mistake to explain uniformity in housing in this way, and then to conclude that we follow 'the demands of the times', because we are tied to modern production methods. On the contrary, modern production methods have nothing to do with it. MH, even if carried out by the most primitive means, will still bear all the characteristics of uniformity. We see it as much in its traditional forms as in the most sophisticated prefabrication methods of present-day MH.

Nature knows no uniformity, but seeks ever greater variety.

21

Uniformity may therefore be seen as *unnatural* in the sense that it is an artificial phenomenon. In this way MH as we see it today is unnatural because it is an artificial way of housing. The provision of dwellings by means of MH is an artificial imitation of the housing process as it would be if the natural relationship were in operation. MH is the result of this imitation. It is not the result of the growing process of a living organism, but at most the result of a lively industry. It differs from the town we need as a plastic flower differs from a real one.

MH is the realisation of the question asked by builders, architects, economists and numerous others: what should a modern dwelling look like? It is not the result of any quest for a way of *bringing the housing process to life*. That is why the MH city is only representative in the eyes of these professional groups and for authorities, but it does not represent its population, although one might have expected that to have been put first.

Let us assume for a moment that the form of contemporary dwelling is representative of the life it contains. This would indicate that uniformity is characteristic of modern society. What would that mean?

We cannot deny the right to exist to groups in society which assume the signs of uniformity. Our present society may, from certain points of view, be seen as existing for such groups. But we can at once add this observation: that uniformity will always mean an emphasis on the greatest common factor.

Uniformity is a sign of voluntary or involuntary incorporation. A man who puts on a uniform does so to serve; he is an instrument by means of which a purpose is to be attained, whereby an organisation seeks to achieve something. To choose a uniform will therefore mean to take sides. It means that one wishes to isolate, in a group, from everyday life, and a uniform affords the opportunity to a kind of collective exclusiveness in which a large part of its attraction is to be found. To lend sense to a uniform one always needs an outer world. The uniform group places itself apart, and wants to carve out a small world from the larger world of every day. This shows also the artificiality of the uniform. It means the making of an invented world and invented relationships.

When we want to make up a separate world from the larger, varied world, this happens more or less in the same way as an image is carved from a block of wood. We give form by removing something. By cutting away those parts which constitute variety we are left with certain common characteristics which determine the form of the uniform expression. The monastery and the garrison are among such little worlds. Their purpose may be totally different, but both come about by applying the same manipulations by which normal life is restricted. The artificial world of a uniformed society is thus always a limited one, and joining it always means making a choice.

How can these characteristics of purpose and restriction be reconciled with a society which is to be housed? For this society does not exist to fulfil a purpose in the sense referred to above. In the framework of our subject it may be assumed that society is to be housed without conditions: its existence itself is its purpose. We are concerned with the ordinary, total world itself, out of which all those little worlds of limitations and purposes can be carved. *Man's way of living is the most ordinary thing in the world.* It is daily life in all its richness, the inexhaustible source from which our intelligence may fabricate artificial little worlds by leaving out the varieties and emphases of common life.

If the form of dwelling today is representative of our daily life, if this form is a reflection of the ordinary and the normal, then we encounter a contradiction. It would mean that the common has become special, and the normal exceptional. Of course, we cannot accept that. Society has not become unnatural but the housing of society is no longer representative, and we can therefore derive from the mass housing town no understanding of the people living there. The form of housing we supply for ourselves conforms to an invented, restricted world, and has thus indeed become barrack living, and in comparison with the inexhaustible variety of real existence can therefore be called unnatural to a high degree.

An emergency measure

This remarkable phenomenon in contemporary life allows us to see clearly the true nature of MH, and thus to understand why, while in itself appearing to be so reasonable and normal, its consistent application has given rise to such disturbing results. We have seen how the artificial condition which arises when the action of the individual is excluded is not *in itself* unacceptable. Uniformity becomes objectionable only when it no longer restricts itself to the separation of a part of society, but wishes to encompass the whole. Now that MH is applied almost exclusively, the bounds of toleration have long been passed, and the process of the natural relationship, the source of a living community, has dried up. A housing process which rests upon this natural relationship can well absorb a certain

23

amount of MH, but as the application of the method grows the process itself is affected and finally stifled. A new phase is thus entered which we are now experiencing, a phase where we can no longer speak of a housing process, but merely an organised *sheltering* of people. MH may be a good way of sheltering a large number of people, but it is not the means of housing which any society should adopt and it is by this latter criterion that we must judge the method. We thus come to this remarkable paradox that MH is inadmissible as soon as the question of housing on a massive scale is raised.

In fact, MH in its original conception was never intended to house the entire community. It was merely an emergency measure which was seized upon when the normal process fell short. It was a means which was useful when a large number of people had to be sheltered in a short space of time. It was used when for various reasons the natural relationship had already been interrupted, and when certain groups of people for one reason or another could not house themselves—groups which thanks to this method were at any rate saved from homelessness. The paupers who originally were housed in this way were paupers just because they had no place in the normal pattern; because they had become isolated from it; and had to be housed by external measures, by an artificial effort. MH has indeed been a blessing in recent times for countless people, and as an emergency measure has contributed to the fact that our civilisation has survived the industrial revolution. *But our problem began when this emergency measure from the turn of the century grew into housing for the entire community, and thus became the norm.* This explains how it occurred that MH had been applied for so long before a sense of unease and anxiety made itself felt.

We are therefore in a period of transition. We must not rely for too long on this emergency measure, any more than we must take too much of a necessary medicine. We have to find our way back to the production of a normal diet. It is as if our housing is suspended in the air for a moment, away from human reality. In this brief moment we will have to find the means and organisation to get the natural process going again, this time enriched with techniques and technical experience we have gathered during the last sixty-odd years. If we do not succeed in this soon our housing problems will overwhelm us because of the unnaturalness of our solution. Instead of concerning ourselves in ever greater panic with the emergency measure we must turn towards the healthy organism which has been threatened by too severe a medicine.

24

Brick-and-mortar statistics

It is the uniformity of modern neighbourhoods rather than any other consequence of MH which awakens the opposition of the public. Therefore most attacks are directed to this phenomenon, so much so that the symptom and not the disease is treated. Uniformity is accepted as inevitable, as long as it is not too universal. A compromise is therefore sought which will affect the efficacy of the system as little as possible but reduces the amount of uniformity. This is where the conflict arises between life and method—a conflict which was already noted by Van der Waerden and which is still raging.

It does not seem improbable that we could build enough dwellings by allowing MH its head strictly according to the laws of the method. If the number of dwelling types is drastically limited, built in strict uniformity throughout the land, and with all details and materials centrally distributed, it would undoubtedly result in a considerable increase in production. But although this objective was first formulated decades ago, the execution of this programme has as yet not met with success. Indeed, it has not even been seriously attempted because it is clear that something would result which even on the most superficial consideration would be opposed to what may be expected of a town or of housing. Evidently human instinct revolts against the consequences of the method and thus prevents us reaping the benefits in terms of productivity of an emerging measure which was adopted in the first place because of its productivity potential.

The interruption of the natural relationship has not resulted in a situation where the inhabitants are no longer a hindrance to building activity; it appears indeed that they are the only hindrance. Thus each well-meaning attempt to meet the desire for variation in daily life appears as a concession to inefficiency and an encroachment upon the chosen work method. On the other hand the gain to the inhabitants is minimal, because the unnatural situation of which uniformity is a symptom has not changed. The natural relationship has not been restored; the only result is a greater number of small series of uniform dwellings instead of a few large ones.

Even to those who only wish to see housing in terms of production all this should be worth considering; evidently MH is only in theory capable of providing large-scale housing because this theory by definition does not take into account the one factor which inhibits the production of MH, namely the user with his stubborn desire for variety. But to lay bare completely the paradox of MH we must realise that on the one hand it demands concrete form which shall provide man's housing needs, once and for all; and that at the same time MH demands that projects are fashioned which are representative of those who live in them! When a MH builder has to design an estate for a few hundred workers' families he can move in two directions. He can, as we saw, inquire into what functions a worker's dwelling has to fulfil, and go out to collect information and call in statistical research. But he can also shut his eyes and try to envisage what a worker's dwelling, *the* worker's dwelling, should look like, what *he* thinks an estate for a few hundred workers' families should look like. Usually both approaches are adopted, roughly in the order given. In both cases in fact the same question is asked: the quest for 'the dwelling'. MH demands a design which is representative for people as yet unknown who will inhabit it, but MH also demands, and this above all, uniformity which can never be representative of the life to be established.

Again and again can we see MH as a frenzied attempt to make matter conform to people, and again and again it turns out to be MH itself which prevents people from identifying with matter.

MH wants massive housing, but society can only tolerate this on a very limited scale.

MH seeks a form which is a perfect representation of the life contained in it, but at the same time aims at the most rigid uniformity.

The idea that matter is to be formed in harmony with the people to be housed also means that the town resulting from it should be in conformity with the community living in it. Building has therefore to be carried out in such a way that the community, once admitted to the productions, is not forced to assume an unnatural form. Society should not be contorted to fit in a MH district. This notion also is made impossible by the method itself.

Are not statistics perhaps the prime means to ensure harmony with society? Statistics enable us to acquire an insight into very complex phenomena. To understand for example how the population of the country is composed we divide it into groups and determine their size by counting. It is clear that these groups themselves are chosen with an eye on the purpose in mind. People are divided according to belief, income, race, age, etc. These groups of course have no existence in group form, in that their component individuals cannot be observed together as a group. But only by studying such information can an insight be gained into a real situation. If I have a handful of beads of different colours, I can get an idea of what I have got by dividing the beads into groups so that each group has more or less the same colour. But one thing is certain: the real situation is always different from the one that emerges after my arrangement.

It can be quite useful, then, to divide the population into imaginary groups. But the tragedy of MH is that it is far more suitable for such *imaginary* groups than for the complex, varied reality. MH wants to do no more than make series of similar units, and to that end it is much easier to give form to the artificial statistical image than investigate the nature of a real situation.

Thus we see brick-and-mortar statistics arising throughout the country, and we can distinguish blocks for bachelors, small families, large families, incomplete families, old people, social misfits, working women, old couples and artists. As with my handful of beads we may be sure that society, by itself, would never arrange itself in such a way. The question is not what sort of arrangement would be better, *but that with* MH *evidently only an arrangement is possible which is not naturally found in society*. That is to say: matter is not manipulated in harmony with society, but society is forced to conform to a method which pretends to perform this task. Again we face a paradox in MH.

Town and population

Perhaps it sounds somewhat pompous to say 'let us form matter in harmony with man, and towns in conformity with the population'. We must remember that a mere poetic statement of an intention regarding housing is not enough. The problem we are wrestling with is that we must achieve this harmony in the most literal sense. There is a great difference between an architect deciding to design a building for a particular activity 'in conformity with the character and nature of that activity' and a town and its population being in harmony with each other. And in this latter case any attempt on the part of MH to create towns in harmony with their population may be well-intentioned but is none the less absurd. On the other hand, if MH turns out to be the wrong method to bring about this harmony between man and matter, that is not to say that we can find a different *method* which would ensure this objective. For there is no reason to suppose that it is ever possible, whatever the method, for matter to conform to society in the sense meant here.

27

By saying that we wish to achieve such a harmony we accept without question that society is a tangible phenomenon having a form which, by observation and design, we can translate into brick and concrete, like a bespoke suit of clothes. This is a very doubtful proposition. It assumes that town and population are two separate quantities which could each assume a form independently of each other, and that it should be possible to create a town form matching that of society. But can anyone imagine a town without a population, or a population without a town? How are we to think of such a population, as a kind of larva-like object? A population without a town is a horde of homeless creatures, formless as water. A town without a population is no more than a collection of buildings doomed to decay.

To arrive at better housing we must begin by refusing to separate town and population, for the form of one determines the form of the other, and consequently the form of the one cannot exist before that of the other. A town is not a thing without people; a town is man and matter together. This concept is related to live and dead matter at the same time. The notion that there can be talk of two quantities can arise only because it fits into the concept behind MH. If a town is created before there is a population this fatal separation is implied.

Then how are we to see this duality of a town?

We encounter the same concept which we met in discussing dwelling. It appeared there that MH is preoccupied with the form of the dwelling; with the dwelling as tangible phenomenon. This notion ran aground on the imaginary functionalism from which 'the dwelling' was to emerge. We decided then to forget about the form for the time being, because this will always be the resultant of certain forces, and proposed to approach the dwelling *from inside* these forces themselves. The dwelling therefore became the result of a relationship of forces between man and matter. An investigation of this play of forces yielded the idea of the natural relationship, and it became clear that MH inevitably had to concern itself with a form because the natural relationship was interrupted.

In the same way we had better not try directly to question the form of the town, but rather the relationship between people and matter which is what the town consists of. The town, as a unity of man and matter, can only be imagined as the result of a process in which the natural relationship takes part, for only then do town and population 'possess' each other to their fullest extent. It is possible then that society, via the individual as its smallest unit, via the dwelling as the smallest unit of the town, can project itself directly into the form of the town. The movement of population and town is then like the movement of a hand kneading a lump of clay. A town, through the functioning of the natural relationship, is an organism in which each cell contains life, an organism that is never complete, but constantly renews itself and grows, ever different and ever the same. A town is a unique phenomenon which grows and flowers in an eternal cycle; a phenomenon in which matter assumes something of the mobility of life, and life receives something of the eternal quality of matter. By seeing the town as a unity it becomes clear that the natural relationship plays a vital part in the housing of man.

The translators of form

But today we no longer think of the town as a unity with people, and when we should do all we can to stimulate a process, we spend our efforts in trying to reflect the form of the population in matter. We are very busy arranging in advance conformity of towns with their future populations because we do not understand that a town, a real town, can only emerge when this conformity already *exists*, and that it cannot be achieved by *making* a town, however beautifully or skilfully.

The people who have to form matter at the behest of MH are the town planner and the architect. They are the translators of form. To see how the disappearance of the natural relationship has muddled all relationships of forces in housing, an observation of these two important elements in the system will be useful. For it is only possible to see clearly the difference between architect and town planner, both form givers but of a very different nature, in the light of the natural relationship. As soon as this relationship is broken, there is hardly any difference between the activities of these two experts, for what the architect does is in essence the same as what the town planner does, and vice versa.

When the natural relationship functions, it is the architect who provides the contact with the occupier. He it is who as expert makes the connection between the natural relationship and a complex technology: he is the direct link between layman and profession. In other words in the natural relationship the architect finds himself in the centre of the housing process; he is part of it. The process operates as much because of him as due to the initiative and interference of the layman.

The town planner, on the other hand, always stands outside the process. Indeed, because of this he is a town planner. He guides the process, canalises it and sets the limits within

29

which it can take place. He is the gardener who guides the growth of the organism and stimulates it by several means. He trims and gives direction to future development, he has to consider the whole. No doubt the organism of the town would grow and live without the town planner, but the result would be chaotic, and the growth would soon be stifled.

When, however, the natural relationship is broken the town planner can no longer guide a living organism, for he has to occupy himself with devising forms which formerly came about *without* him, by means of different forces. In the practice of MH he has to lay down the form and size of blocks of dwellings. Then he enters the domain of the architect, for this activity would not be possible without a clear architectural concept. Once arrived at this position he can no longer find a point where his influence ceases. It would be merely a logical extension of his activities if he proceeded to design the entire town, with all its dwellings and buildings, to the last detail. The gardener no longer finds a plant to be tended, but feels obliged first to imagine the plant, and then to design it. For has not the town then simply become one gigantic design? The town planner no longer gives form to something living, he just makes forms and then has to attempt to breathe life into them. It is a task which since *Pygmalion* has been vouchsafed to no mortal.

The architect also, for his part, can no longer define the nature and range of his work. As soon as he sets out to design a MH project he becomes a town planner. If he follows the logical consequences of MH, his housing project will tend to become bigger and bigger. For the greater the series, the greater the economy. The method leads directly to the idea that one very large building can house an entire district. The architect dreams of the building which is in fact a whole town. And why shouldn't he when the system does not permit him to give some measure of independence to even the smallest unit? On his part then the architect strays as easily into the realm of the town planner, as the town planner is tempted to design dwellings.

From whichever standpoint we approach this state of affairs, it must occur to us that it would be simplest if one man designed the lot. When we start with the assumption that a town is no more than an architectural brief which only requires that people are to be sheltered, there seems no reason to leave its design to several influences.

When we talk about a balanced play of forces in our housing we mean that each force should operate fully without damaging the whole, because its position in relation to the others would by itself ensure the balance. An architect who deals with a living person as client will find a guarantee in this contact that his design will be in harmony with the life which is to be housed. The town planner dealing with a living organism can only succeed if he respects the nature of that organism. This is to say that the form givers can only fully act as form givers because they are constantly in touch with forces which will ensure the harmony towards which all are striving. In MH, however, the form givers can no longer act as such, but can only try not to produce unnatural results. They constantly find that they cannot blindly follow their personal vision without running into the danger of exercising intolerable constraint on innumerable other lives.

The situation created by MH, where on the one hand large numbers are waiting to be housed, and on the other the experts are struggling with the problem how best to effect this, in many ways harbours great dangers. It is not my intention to go into this, but it occurs to me that in a good housing process the craftsman should act as craftsman, the architect as designer, the technician as technician, the user as user, and that it is from the meeting of all these complementary actions that the dwelling and the town must result. All these relationships we do indeed find in the building trade, but not in housing. There is no doubt that the architect has the best intentions at heart when he sets himself to designing a MH project. But in the last instance he can only produce what would be a good MH *project* on the basis of what he knows. And that is not enough, because as provider of housing for other people he is as much a dilettante as they would be if the positions were reversed. His guess, *seen in terms of dwelling*, is no better than that of any layman. The only difference is that he knows about buildings, he can see what is possible technically, economically and aesthetically. The architect is no more capable of solving the riddle by MH (the riddle of *what is a dwelling, what does a town look like?*) than any other mortal; but he is in the position of being able to realise his answer, and the realisation, the building of things which are called dwellings, that is all that MH demands.

Aesthetics and housing

No man is capable of fulfilling the task which MH sets the form givers. But architects and town planners are perhaps less capable of it than most. After all, a town planner is not someone who wants to house society, but to build towns. Similarly the architect has not chosen his profession out of pity for a homeless population, but because he wants to build. There is therefore a good chance that the personal preferences of form givers assume a great influence in their translating. We might even say that the better the architect, the more committed his vision of the architecture of the future, the less he is capable of being guided by other motives. No doubt MH gives the architect the opportunity to conceive projects, and doubtless this fact makes MH attractive to an architectural practitioner. To a genius it gives a chance to commit to paper his whole vision of the city of tomorrow in gigantic architectural projects, and even to carry them to reality; a mediocre talent has an opportunity to produce large building works by the repetition of elements of comparative simplicity in themselves. From an architectural point of view it is nearly always more exciting to build a point block of fifty dwellings than to spread those fifty dwellings in low rise buildings across the ground.

To the form giver every problem is automatically an aesthetic problem, and it is understandable, therefore, that he will see the provision of dwelling from that point of view. Nor is there any objection to this in a housing process made up of well-balanced forces. But because this is not the case in MH it need not surprise us to find that our housing estates are biased towards aesthetic values. This does not mean MH products are always beautiful, but that the attempt is there to *make* them beautiful by approaching them as problems of form.

No living town is beautiful in the way a work of art is. The organism which is a living town may possess the sort of beauty we find in nature, the beauty of plants, rocks, little children and old people: a beauty which is not a matter of proportions or artistic considerations only. When we think a town is beautiful we mean something else; we mean that it has just what we miss in MH districts: that we can identify with it, that in the shape we see we can encounter the inhabitants, that we feel a confrontation with daily life. A town may be beautiful in this way without possessing a single architectural masterpiece. It is an innocent, inevitable beauty.

Dwelling is too ordinary a matter to be called art. As we saw when we considered uniformity, it is a matter-of-course background against which the particular may stand out. A detail, a certain dwelling, a given building, may be a work of art, but housing is not architecture. And just because the form givers have become concerned with housing, has not the odd situation arisen that housing has become a question of architecture?

32

It is difficult to imagine how things could be otherwise in this situation. The creation of towns which are more than considered works of aesthetics is inseparably connected with the natural process. In a subsequent chapter the question will be discussed as to how this process may be brought to life again, and how it will be possible for architects and town planners to turn their full capacities towards achieving more than just aesthetic successes. For the moment it will suffice to point out the remarkable phenomenon that some towns have arisen which can only be appreciated by seeing them as the works of the experts, as compositions of masses, as the outcome of principles and opinions in the sphere of contemporary form giving.

The only way in which a real town can be judged is to identify with it. Fine towns such as have grown in history derive their reputation from the reaction of those who have walked their streets. The town is never seen as a whole, but bit by bit. But if we wish to appreciate the new estates it would be wiser not to visit them, but to unroll the plan. What at first seemed to be a wilful scattering of building blocks without scale will then appear as a clearly ordered division of planes. *The modern town looks best as a model.* The rhythm of the blocks can be admired and the alternation of heights takes on an independent plastic meaning. Indeed, the ultimate realisation of the town planning problem comes about by moving little blocks about on the model. After a lengthy investigation of data and much labour everything falls away but lines, colours and planes. So much has this art developed that such models would make a fine wall decoration, and indeed they are used for that purpose.

All this symbolises the relationship between form givers and users. Does not the method we observe lead straight to the 'great creator' who determines all? Can we wonder that, being human, what he produces is a schematic reduction? Only it is regrettable that the model cannot remain the diagrammatic representation of the direction in which a living process has to grow, but that what we see on the model is literally to be built like that. It is not a diagram, but a design, it is the future of a town, reduced to an enormous architectural sketch, and all the unforeseen happenings which in time will be added to the buildings will be negations of the original vision.

To us all this is important because it is a symbol of a disturbed balance. The town carries the imprint of the influences of which it is made up. The hand of its maker is betrayed everywhere, and because the inhabitants have exercised no

33

influence we encounter only form givers. Never has building been so aesthetically motivated, and never has so much spontaneous beauty been left out. Contemporary neighbourhoods are open-air exhibitions, sample cards of styles and personalities. Even the siting of the blocks contributes to this impression when we note how they place themselves obtrusively in the centre and demand that the pedestrian, as in an exhibition, has carefully to move round them instead of being guided and protected by them on his way through the town.

The blind machine

It begins to look as if architects and town planners take on the mantle of omnipotence because they themselves can now step into the vacuum left by the inhabitant. But this idea is based upon an optical illusion. It seems indeed that the form giver only remains, and wants as it were to perform the housing game in mime. But if initially he seems to have the field to himself, it soon appears that he is not the only one to invade the area abandoned by the inhabitants. He comes across an even stronger opponent than the troublesome client. This opponent is the housing apparatus itself which is insatiable in its urge to produce. An apparatus which calls upon a steady stream of facts, leans upon a shortsighted 'realism'; a realism of numbers of people who have to be housed, statistics of 'dwelling requirements'. This blind machine dominates the scene more and more, and, producing inexorably, steamrollers across open fields, leaving behind ever more lifeless tracts of habitation. It is invulnerable, because it wields two weapons which inspire a pious respect: *technical necessity* and *scientifically justified research*. Against these two even the visionary architect is powerless. The only thing open to him is to seek what variation he may, by a more playful arrangement of blocks or by fumbling impotently with balconies and water spouts.

Thus is the merciless exclusion of the individual accomplished. Not only do the inhabitants disappear from the scene, but also the form giver in any meaningful sense of the word. He no longer goes to the heart of his task, but remains on the outside of a system that maintains itself in a position of sublime indifference.

The rigidity of the mass housing city

The image which MH has of a city as a material form which must be adjusted to a given community is an extremely static one. For MH sees both the town and the community as two separate static quantities. This does not mean that no attempt is made to consider any future developments, but that the method does not permit this to be done in a fruitful way. After all, MH as a means of providing houses is necessarily restricted by the facts known only at the moment the design takes form. MH tries to foresee everything, indeed has to do this, before building can begin, and is therefore incapable of coping with the unforeseen. In order to understand fully the evil results of the absence of the natural relationship it is necessary to judge the town not only as design but also as living phenomenon which is in a constant state of change. We therefore have to see the MH town in relationship to the progress of time.

A town is above all movement; movement of forces of matter and society in a restless process. If, for example, it were possible today to build a gigantic building which could shelter the entire population, there would be no reason to do so. The question we have to ask is how such an enormous object is to maintain itself in time. How will it renew itself? How will it behave to prevent decay? How shall new inventions and changing opinions be incorporated? The test of the ability of a town to cope with time lies in its ability to adapt to change, to assimilate the new, to alter part by part, and yet to maintain its identity, and to ensure its existence and that of its inhabitants without too severe shocks. It is relatively simple to *build* a town, but what shall be done to make it *exist*?

MH is a totality in which it is difficult to change any individual part. Not only is each dwelling irrevocably anchored in the large block but the blocks themselves in their town planning scheme are so arranged that they often form part of a larger series. This makes it difficult, if not impossible, for a neighbourhood to exist organically and allow part after part to change under the impact of life. For decades the district will be inaccessible to such renewals as may be necessary. No new appearance, no new technology, no new amenities, no new concept of living can have their effect on it without reconsidering the whole concern anew as housing project.

Because the users cannot determine what has to be done, little can be changed as a result of their requirements: too bad if they want to enrich their lives, to raise their standards of comfort or establish their social position. Their dwellings will be replaced when they are worn out. *Not* when they are obsolete, *not* when they no longer accord with the accepted opinions about dwelling, *not* when the occupant feels that his facilities compare badly with what is available elsewhere, but *only* when their technical efficiency is impaired to such an extent that they constitute a danger to health. None of the impulses which arise from the natural relationship can be allowed to have their effect.

It is in the nature of the MH idea that when a district is worn out, it is replaced by another MH project. The site is reorganised. The modern town therefore, in contrast with a healthy organism of which all members are the same age, is divided into districts which each have their own degree of decay and usefulness. There will thus always be categories, a hierachy of neighbourhoods. When one part has sunk to its lowest ebb it will suddenly, by a great effort from outside, become the most modern. This means that the kind of place one lives in depends totally upon what district one lives in. The inhabitant is at the mercy of the round of the MH machine which has to build the town anew. There will always be a housing shortage somewhere in the town, which can only be overcome by rebuilding. It is evident that the system which, as we saw, is an emergency measure will itself ensure that there will constantly be an emergency situation somewhere.

This state of affairs may possibly have been accepted in the past when a social hierarchy existed so that the better class would leave an older district to be peopled by a middle class, which in its turn left its cast-offs to the working class. But how can this be reconciled with a society where class differences in this sense are fast disappearing, and a high standard of convenience in dwelling is desirable for all; a society, moreover, where people with similar incomes no longer belong to the same social group? The MH town will have old and new specimens of all kinds of dwellings (for small, medium, incomplete and large families, for old couples, bachelors, working women and artists, workers, middle class, the better-off and whatever more divisions brick-and-mortar statistics have made possible). The new ones will conform in their technolological expertise and finish to the standards of the time; the old ones will not merely be old but irrevocably antiquated because their MH nature will not permit them to move with the times. For each category into which MH has divided society there will be individuals who live in up-to-date or obsolete dwellings: one is lucky or not, and if not, there is little to be done about it. So whether one is rich or poor, prepared to spend some money on one's own dwelling or not, MH will see to it that no gradation of housing standards can exist within the district where one lives. All the occupant can do is to try and move to a better dwelling. *The system therefore invites a constant game of musical chairs.*

36

Housing standards in a MH town can only be on a high level in newly reorganised areas. That is to say that, when a certain technical improvement has become possible, such as better sound insulation or heating systems, these improvements can only be applied in those areas which at that moment happen to be rebuilt. The inhabitants who would readily pay for these novelties can only do anything about it if they manage to secure a dwelling in a new district. The manufacturer of these improvements cannot provide them all over the town but only in the redeveloping areas. He can only hope to have supplied the whole town when his improvements themselves have become obsolete, when the reorganisation cycle is complete. At a time when technological development is in full swing, when improvements closely follow each other, this is an intolerable situation which undoubtedly impedes the technical development of housing. For it means nothing less than that the life span of the dwelling cannot be influenced by new technical possibilities, but depends on the time it takes for the entire building to be worn out. An individual may decide to replace something good by something better (a possibility which the motor car industry has perfected, and which encouraged the rapid development of the motor car) but not where large-scale activities manipulated by MH prevent this.

Experimentation in housing has therefore become a hazardous business. In the natural relationship it may be said that the fact that an occupier who knows what he wants and is prepared to spend money and trouble, and has to live with his mistakes, is to some extent a guarantee against serious failures. A manufacturer can test his product in small-scale experiments. But in MH any novel idea may be applied immediately, on an immense scale and for a long time, before the user comes into contact with it, and therefore before the result of the experiment can be properly tested. The same is true with new ideas in dwelling; improvements relating, say, to partitioning of dwellings in accordance with the evolution of living habits already in progress. A new idea will only be applied slowly and locally. A good idea will be available only to those who live in the latest developments. A bad idea will only slowly be eradicated. A useless idea will persist for the life-span of the building.

Thus MH moves with cumbersome strides from one eruptive renewal to the next, breathlessly plodding behind reality, ever searching and groping, theorising and rationalising in an obstinate attempt to catch up its backlog on life, ever trying to snatch at the incidental and the changeable in collectivities and generalisations.

The modern nomad

The inertia of the MH town brings with it the consequence that *the inhabitants must keep on the move*. Every rebuilding causes migration. The inhabitants move away to new virgin areas, leaving the worn-out ones behind them in a manner which reminds one of primitive tribes who, after exhausting their pasture, move to fresh fields.

Now that the towns have been fully built up, and the first MH estates dating from the turn of the century are ripe for renewal, we are at the beginning of a rebuilding cycle which doubtless will effectively prevent any chance that neighbourhoods and district communities will ever create their own distinctive character.

The conditions which are most favourable for the formation of communities—communities, that is, which are more than a collection of families or individuals—are richly worth studying. We are probably quite capable at the moment of stocking an aquarium in such a way as to create a biological equilibrium, but we have hardly begun to enquire what conditions are necessary for the creation of towns or districts in which *social harmony* may develop. We have not progressed much beyond realising vaguely that this must be a question of organisation, although this is by no means the first priority. In anticipation of a conscious reclamation of this untilled ground I have, I think, incidentally mentioned some conditions which in this respect may be sufficient to throw light once again on the limitations of MH.

The first condition was that of *free combination* by which is meant that as little as possible should be decided in advance as to which families should be housed, and in what order—a decision which, as was shown, becomes steadily more difficult in an evolving society. The brick-and-mortar statistics put forward by MH make an organic mix virtually impossible. They require, if taken to their ultimate conclusion, that a person should move house at each new stage in his life, at each change in the composition of his family.

A second condition is undoubtedly that *the occupant's environment is capable of constant renewal*. This point touches the heart of dissatisfaction with MH. The indifference of MH to the personal initiative of the dweller is the reason that he can never take possession of his environment, but at most can only adapt to what is offered him. The necessity of communal responsibility and a healthy rivalry with neighbouring environments are too evident to be described again.

Finally *time* is a condition of the utmost importance. The formation of a community may be encouraged, but it should never be forced. Undoubtedly more than one generation is required to enable a society to become one with its environment, and to allow the environment in turn to grow into harmony with its people. It is often pointed out, and correctly, that new estates will one day look habitable. But this will take years. In the meantime something has to happen, and as we see time passing over MH districts all we notice is decay. Time is required so that the natural relationship, in its constant and involuntary activity, will fill out and refine the necessarily diagrammatic situation. It is necessary that during this time the district can renew itself in its parts, and can change from detail to detail. If this does not happen we shall see such absurdities as trees, planted when the scheme was new, just reaching maturity by the time the district is to be rebuilt.

People require more time to grow into a community than it takes MH to wear out. A district with character will therefore in MH always be a slum. We have become so used to this that character and personality in a district are almost instinctively associated in our minds with a certain degree of decay, with the melancholy of age. Therefore the task we have to set ourselves, if we wish that the society of the future can really identify itself with its town and yet maintain its standards of comfort, is quite unique: *We have to make possible the creation of districts which may grow old without becoming obsolete, which can absorb the latest ideas and yet have a sense of history. Districts in which the population can live for generations, and which yet incorporate the potential for change.* This is the opposite of what MH offers us.

The contemporary town dweller is a nomad who moves from place to place without taking part in the growth of his environment, just as he does not have to reproach himself with its poverty. He experiences his town as something outside himself and finds his self-expression, entirely in conformity with his nomadic existence, in his motor car. We have indeed come a long way from the man we imagined at the beginning: a man who creates his environment in harmony with himself.

THE TECHNIQUE

Questions and possibilities

After our first cursory consideration of the natural relationship between man and his dwelling, and the unsatisfying situation in which MH places him, a wider view may now be taken. The behaviour of the occupant is of such practical consequence that one must ask why its importance has not been recognised before now, and why, at any rate in housing studies, it has not been taken into account more consciously? In reply one may suggest that, being rational to a high degree, MH has its own logic. Often, therefore, it is difficult to accept that objections against contemporary housing are its direct result. One is inclined to see these objections as merely illogical. Only when it is made clear that the logic of MH exists outside the reality of life, and that *any* application of it is in conflict with life, will its stranglehold be broken.

But what then? If this argument is pursued to its logical conclusion, we must review not only our towns, but our entire thought pattern about building and dwelling. To make this possible and arrive at something better we must first convince ourselves of the failure of mass housing, and in particular, isolate the essential elements of modern reality. It is time, then, to distinguish between what *is* possible and what *should be* possible, and to answer numerous questions which doubtless will arise at this point in the argument, especially those which will sharpen this insight. Indeed much is possible, for if we can see the situation in terms of a balance of forces one of which is missing, it only remains to reinstate this force. Such an attempt can hardly be called destructive or negative. The forces already existing are in no way affected: our capacity for organisation, our constructive and technological ability, our skill in research and experiment, in perfection and execution—all these matters on which we pride ourselves and which we apply to mass housing with such little success. Contrary to some expectations they will be spurred on to greater and

40

more effective action by the addition of the missing force. The introduction of the natural relationship could be the catalyst. It is in this positive direction that we must turn our thoughts.

The natural relationship more than ever necessary

The decision to reintroduce the natural relationship in housing is justified not only by arguments put forward in the previous chapters. The direction in which the relationship between man and dwelling is developing today shows the determined action of the natural relationship ever more necessary.

The whole of social development is directed to an increase in the personal rights of man. How can this democratic process tally with a method of housing more akin to totalitarianism in its actions and forms? In Berlage's day the workers were not unjustified in showing instinctive and violent reaction against the wide application of mass housing. They demanded for themselves the rights enjoyed by the middle and upper classes. Nowadays everyone has reason to complain that all 'classes' are housed in a manner violently resented by an earlier generation. But the question deals with more than the rights of individual man: it also deals with *duties*. The acquisition of a free citizen's rights involves a concurrent burden of responsibility. It is very questionable whether society can permit the responsibility for housing to be taken out of the hands of the individual. Just as a democracy cannot assume the responsibility for bringing up children without damaging itself severely, the problem of housing cannot be dumped on a technical-organisational apparatus. The ultimate care for the development of a child rests with the parents (albeit with the help of schools and educational institutions) and the centre of gravity of the housing process must lie in the same hands. People should be given all possible help in the execution of their task, but it is decidedly wrong to relieve them of it altogether. The natural relationship is as essential a key to individual responsibility as it is to the unfolding of certain forces in the housing process. It assumes that the individual will take possession of his environment, and what does that mean but the acceptance of responsibility? There is, then, a clear contradiction between mass housing and the self-awareness of society. It is possible to defend mass housing with conviction, but this inevitably leads one into conflict with the fundamental nature of society.

If it is our serious intent to create a society in which the individual has increasing opportunity to evolve his potential, the relationship between man and dwelling must become more direct. The *opposite* of mass housing should be our aim. The relationship between man and dwelling, formerly the exclusive privilege of its better-situated members, must become a universal right. Increasing leisure time and a rising standard of living will develop in the broad mass of the population activities and interests, until recently the province of the few. Thus it is increasingly difficult to make assumptions about a collective pattern of behaviour as characterising a particular income group. Mass housing needs such a pattern to be effective and therefore stumbles on the impossibility of forming a reasonably accurate idea of the behaviour and desires of a certain group. The average working-class family has long since ceased to exist. In the broad layers of our population a multi-directional development is taking place, which, for the time being, does not set recognisable patterns, and will certainly not do so in the near future. It is therefore illusory to believe that the blunt measures of mass housing can determine dwelling types without damaging this development. Who is to say how the living patterns of different layers of society will shape in the future? Even within the same income group there are many families and individuals with widely differing backgrounds, ambitions and living habits. How can mass housing deal with that?

The unknown as basis

The result of these reflections must be that, when considering housing of the future, we should not try to forecast what will happen, but try to *make provision for what cannot be foreseen*. The uncertainty of the future itself must be the basis on which present decisions are taken. Without this point of departure every prognosis is worthless, for it is exactly what we cannot foresee which is most characteristic of the future, not the straight extension of the present. But how is it possible to take measures today which will also prove effective for the unforeseen situations of the distant future?

Mass housing attempts to grapple with the unknown by carefully calculating future trends. Such a strategy is essential for its operation, but sooner or later it will have to be revised when confronted with the unforeseen. If at that moment we have nothing but an obsolete plan at our disposal, only two alternatives remain: either we restate the whole problem, of which the old strategy was the outcome, and start again from the ground up in the certainty that upon its completion our new plan will have been overtaken by further unforeseen circumstances; or we must revise the existing plan piecemeal without any clear criteria, trusting to luck that as much as possible of the original conception is retained.

Of course it is necessary to make plans for the future, and the more exact the better. But that by itself is not enough. Every plan is open to criticism, and is as changeable as the planners themselves. In addition, every attempt to make provision for the future in the sense described above, will necessarily mean a restriction of what is possible: a diagrammatic reduction of many-faceted reality is inevitable.

How can we take hold of our environment, and of life itself, without betraying its complexity and immense potential? This is basic to approaching the future with open eyes and it is the dilemma we must solve in our housing.

So it is not sufficient to have a plan. A plan has value only if it is based on certain clear rules of the game. These rules are required to solve the housing problem in principle, so that any further action will not resurrect the whole problem or confront us with other questions of principle. If we could act in accordance with a set of rules, emerging from the relationship of forces in our existence we should indeed participate in a contemporary culture without troubling whether we 'act in accordance with our time'. We could then talk about a solution for our needs in principle.

Mass housing does not give rules for a *game* but rules for *life*. In undertaking a mass housing project one proceeds in the manner of an officer preparing a parade. The complex figures which the troops will execute must be carefully prepared. Everything has to be foreseen to the last detail. The sudden eruption of an unforeseen circumstance is a disaster which will destroy the total image irrevocably. We can understand the leader's anxiety that one of the soldiers might suddenly act on his own. When that happens he loses his grip on the whole. The unexpected spontaneity of life must be excluded at all costs.

If, however, one wants a number of people to move about a field in an orderly manner, without excluding the spontaneity of life, one must hold not a parade but a game. To play a game is to take into account precisely the unexpected. Its rules are based on the idea that ever-changing variety is possible, that the unexpected will take place, and that surprises will manifest themselves. If, therefore, we introduce the natural relationship into housing, this should have the effect of throwing a football into a group of parading soldiers. The resulting game of football undoubtedly will be the despair of the sergeant-major, who sees only the destruction of his plans. In reality however a new order will have been achieved in life: an order in which the unforeseen can take its place.

The most weighty argument for re-introducing the natural relationship is the need to come to terms with the future. It is self-evident that a game can only succeed through the active participation of all its players. Disregard the desire for amenities and the user's right to have his say; disregard the necessity of having the user as antagonist in a healthy building process; disregard the degree of responsibility which the user shoulders in the concern for dwelling; it is simply impossible even to start providing for the future if a powerful functioning of the natural relationship is not placed first.

If this is so, and we wish to trace those things which are necessary to begin work successfully, it is clear that neither architectural plans nor town-planning schemes are essential. We are not concerned in the first place with designing a town, but with creating rules for a game designed to make creativity possible. This leads us to understand why architects and town-planners in spite of their stubborn and often idealistic aspirations to solve a need, have not succeeded. The problem requires us to leave the expert field and boldly enter an area where all are dilettanti: human life in all its implications.

The unknown missing factor

It is high time to mention technology and, in particular, modern machine-production technology. So far I have deliberately refrained from mentioning this because the housing problem is not in the first instance a technical one. The mass housing idea however, bases itself on certain questionable conceptions about modern technology and we shall not arrive at any better answer unless these conceptions are examined. The development of mass housing may be seen partly as the outcome of a fatal misconception concerning the role of technics at this point in time. In this connexion we are not so much concerned with the idea of technology as exact calculable science, but with opinions, judgments and prejudices which are held about technology and which now determine our actions and thoughts. Once again, a paradoxical situation may be noted in the relationship between technology and mass housing.

If there is one indisputable fact it is the growth of our technical capacity. Our housing problem therefore cannot be of a technical nature! I am not thinking only of contemporary housing techniques, for this rather makes us suspect a certain anaemia, but of our entire arsenal of technical capabilities: the total potential of knowledge and experience from which housing may also expect to profit. It is remarkable that despite the fantastic development of this mighty weapon, we have lost confidence in it as a means of making the natural relationship work with proper power. It has never been suggested that our technical ability should be directed to this end. It has always gone unquestioned that mass housing should be justified by technical considerations only.

Considering its history it may be felt that I am idealising the natural relationship, and, that is free, general operation must be rejected as a utopian dream never yet realised. It cannot be denied however that the natural relationship represents an obvious position from which we instructively take our departure, and that in retrospect the ideal apparently was not achieved because unwieldy, intractable matter could not follow life's capricious turns directly and flexibly. Slow and clumsy technology was the weak link in housing dynamics, though admittedly, the pace of life was slower. Whatever the case, it was not the human situation which obstructed a free intercourse between man and matter, but the technical solutions which were available.

The paradoxical situation I hinted at is this: at the very moment in history when technology is embarking upon enormous development and, for the first time, it seems possible to allow the natural relationship to function better than ever before, attention is being turned instead towards a totally different end: the natural relationship is being broken consciously with definite arguments. Now that a powerful organisational capacity has been developed, and no technical demands appear too great or too complex, the problem with which history has grappled, for better or worse, is held to be insoluble: so insoluble that it is not even posed.

This contradiction becomes even more pointed when we contemplate the development of people and nations who seek liberation and announce equal rights for all, who imagine themselves masters of the material world and strive to extend the privileges of the few to all men. This tendency aims at the fullest operation of the natural relationship on a hitherto unimagined scale, and leads me to put forward this so-called 'utopia' as a necessity and to use it as criterion.

A careful historical investigation could certainly suggest a reason for this. But even without that, it may be possible to understand how the twin streams of social development and housing, could flow in diametrically opposed directions. MH is an emergency measure *par excellence*. In order to provide shelter and amenities for large masses of people, the method is exploited to the utmost. This initial application of MH is understandable but its status as an emergency measure has been forgotten, together with the idea that the natural relationship is closely associated with the well-being of town and society.

To be aware that something is missing one must first know that it does in fact exist. In the past, human housing was based so obviously on the natural relationship that, although deviation may have occurred in practice, the fact was not consciously recognised. It could not be foreseen that the non-functioning of the natural relationship in housing would be disagreeable for the individual, and would actually endanger the very foundation of the housing process.

In one respect this problem has a parallel in beri-beri, a disease which manifested itself in Java after the first world war. The disease had not been previously noticed and, as doctors had no idea of its origins, it spread rapidly. About this time, the large-scale production of white rice had been undertaken. Before this, rice consumed by the population had been divested of its indigestible outer husk by an age-old process, which retained a thin reddish membrane round the kernel. Modern techniques facilitated the building of enormous factories for skinning red rice by a mechanical process which also removed the thin red membrane. Thus a palatable yet inexpensive white rice was made available to the entire population. After much research, the inexplicable disease turned out to be the result of this 'improvement'. It was shown that the red membrane contained certain foodstuffs indispensable to a people relying on rice for its main nourishment. It was the discovery of vitamins.

A blind belief

The story of beri-beri has another parallel with that of MH. The cause of the disease lay in a quarter where it was least expected. Vitamins were found in a component part which was discarded in the genuine belief that an important improvement in people's food was being effected. Previously people had been spared the disease because technology had not been developed sufficiently for the large-scale production of white rice. In a sense the disease resulted from the creation of a technical possibility.

Is not the position of MH such that we have only recently

attained housing on a massive scale by means of technology and organisation? Only now is it possible to stamp entire towns out of the ground through the medium of gigantic designs. Our era is the first to cherish the illusion that total MH is feasible, because on technical grounds it cannot be shown impossible. To house an entire population, to provide it with comfortable dwellings (whatever dwelling may be)—that is the dream of our generation. At a stroke, by establishing a techno-organisational apparatus, it must be possible to accomplish universally, quickly and perfectly what formerly had to be started individually, hesitantly and wretchedly, over and over again. How clever and powerful we are, to have succeeded for the first time in history in bringing together all the cumbersome plurality of un-coordinated labour in terms of productivity! The definition of this task is so simple. To a generation primarily concerned with maintaining its momentum all this is sufficient inducement to carry on blindly. It then surprises us to find that although we are able to undertake immense engineering projects, lay out extensive road systems and send millions of soldiers all over the globe, the building of a simple housing estate refuses to meet with success.

Perhaps it is superfluous to repeat that, as an emergency measure, MH has performed invaluable service, and is still doing so. An automatism, however, manifests itself in our housing which can be explained only in terms of our bewitchment by partially-understood technical possibilities. Only a generation which has stared itself blind upon the technical and organisational aspects of the housing problem, can now realise with astonishment that it never considered an alternative solution.

Machine production

It is only a matter of time before attention is deflected from MH: soon it will become clear that even from the technical point of view the method is no longer so attractive. This development cannot be far distant, for after all, is not MH the product of the pre-machine age? Not only is the method conceptually out of place in our time, but technically it has fallen behind. Contrary to popular opinion, MH can hardly be adapted to the mass-production principles which today serve us so well.

The notion that MH is in technical accord with factory production rests on a misconception. It is generally agreed that the elimination of the individual makes machine mass production possible. This elimination brings important results, because, runs the argument, the system must also increase production in housing. An association of ideas is thus set up regarding machine production. The elimination of the individual in MH however, by no means entails the introduction of the machine. The result is a series of uniform dwellings and although machine production is indeed geared to uniform objects, what has a factory to do with uniform dwellings? There is a fundamental difference between uniform dwellings and factory products.

The mass-produced factory article is moved along a production line, from one operation to the next. That is to say, the apparatus stands still, but the article moves about. But in the building of dwellings, whether produced in series or not, it is the apparatus which moves about, and the product which stands still. The factory, therefore, is not capable of producing entirely finished dwellings, and consequently it does not care whether dwellings are uniform or not. The factory, however, can make parts and elements, and therefore it is very concerned whether such housing components can be made in large uniform series. In other words: *it does not matter to the factory what dwellings look like, whether they are uniform or not, as long as the parts can be made in series which are large enough for us to talk about factory mass-production. This requirement* MH *cannot fulfil.*

MH tries to combine the building of many dwellings into one large project, but as we have already noticed, society objects to excessively large series. Series, therefore, will be always limited in size: too small in themselves to make factory production of parts a viable proposition. MH looks to the single project only: each separate undertaking is different from the others. Every series is a new design, made up from several new details and elements, and no factory can constantly adapt itself to each new series. Thus the factory method remains largely outside housing.

When a MH project makes its series large enough to justify factory production of elements, a uniformity results of such severity that it becomes intolerable. MH and machine thus cannot be reconciled. There is no question of adaptation for we can aim at full factory production of housing components only when the dwellings themselves no longer need to be produced in uniform series. In designing housing then, one must take into account the potential of the machine, and consider the consequence mentioned above. One of the many paradoxes of MH is that although uniformity is characteristic of this type of building, a variety of juxtaposed techniques, constructions and details is used. MH, the thought process behind it all, is anything but uniform. In the same neighbourhood each block may display its own construction method, its own details, its own products, its own ways of building. Certainly, many industrially-produced elements are employed, but the general composition of the blocks is the result of preference, experience and personal ideas on the part of architects and building contractors, and betrays no evidence of a building method thoughtfully based on factory production.

The machine is capable of producing uniform elements which —given they are part of a coherent system—allow an infinite variety of forms. MH, however, by suppressing this variety, does not guarantee such a coherent system. Nor need this surprise us, for MH is not based upon a philosophy of construction but on a method of operation. In the days when this emergency measure was applied with success, industrial production, in the form we now know it, did not exist, and the only way of increasing productivity was by regulating as efficiently as possible what took place on the building site itself. As repetition unquestionably works quicker than a sequence of different actions, it was decided to organise each project, as far as possible, into simple and repetitive actions. That is how the uniform dwelling arose. Undoubtedly it is much simpler for the contractor and his workmen to build the same dwelling ten times over than to build ten different ones. MH was, therefore, an extreme effort to increase production in a world without the machine; an effort which was possible only by the interruption of the relationship between man and dwelling. The whole approach to giving form to our housing is shot through with this obsolete method and it is no use trying to adapt it to the machine. It is senseless to try and use as many industrial products as possible in this system, for to gain full advantage of machine production *we must start from the production end to arrive at a suitable method of operation*, instead of stubbornly sticking to the MH method. As long as this does not happen our efforts in housing will be as equivocal as if the motor car industry were to attempt the production of seventeenth-century coaches by a factory mass-production system.

The dream of producing completely factory-made houses, more or less as motor cars are produced, is already a fairly old one. Although pointing out that MH does not allow full mechanisation of housing because its philosophy does not take into account the role of the machine and factory production, it does not mean that I am advocating this dream-house. The comparison with such technical success as that of the motor car industry is too glib and far too misleading. Once again we find ourselves searching for 'the dwelling', the thing to be designed, the Liberating Object, and this is exactly the road which is closed to us, even if we imagine that in seeking the mechanically-produced dwelling, we move with the times. It does not matter whether at this moment it is decided exactly how the mechanisation of the dwelling is to be accomplished: what matters is that mechanical production is by no means synonymous with MH, and that it should be possible to exploit the machine fully without ending up with MH. The machine in no way implies uniform dwellings and uniform ways of living: it has its own laws. It is curious that no one has ever tried to evolve a housing process based on the machine production system. So far in this respect, all attempts have proceeded from a belief that MH should result, which is quite a different matter. The mechanisation of housing, of which we have heard so much, is nothing but an attempt to mechanise *mass* housing. We are, however, investigating conditions for the healthy functioning of a housing process, and at this stage, all we know about the machine is that it does not automatically presuppose MH. This is important, for it gives us an assurance that the machine may be fully involved in the housing process, and can therefore free us from our last hesitation in rejecting MH.

In other words, we know now that the reintroduction of the natural relationship does not conflict with machine production: it is only in conflict with MH.

Prefabrication

In distinguishing what is part of MH and what is not, prefabrication must be mentioned, for numerous prefabrication systems have supplemented other attempts to make housing on the one hand more productive and on the other, better integrated with the machine. In itself prefabrication means no more than the manufacture of housing components in one place and their assembly in another. It does not therefore necessarily mean machine production, for the work method used may be primitive or hard labour. Prefabrication is thus no more the outcome of the mechanical process than MH. The method arises when conditions for manufacture on the site are unfavourable. At the time of the great gold rush, for example, large numbers of prefabricated wooden houses were shipped to California. The enormous influx of prospectors there had resulted in a great housing shortage, and there were neither carpenters nor carpenters' shops to turn the available wood into houses.

Prefabrication is not necessarily cheaper: transport costs

and the high standard of precision and exact preparation essential for its success could increase prices considerably. In general, the success of the method depends upon a combination of local, economic and labour factors. Nor does prefabrication itself necessarily influence the speed of production favourably. Certainly the amount of on-site work is much less, and the results more spectacular, but total efficiency in this respect is determined by the way the operation in the workshop is prepared and undertaken.

The idea of prefabrication rests on a conviction that work can be produced more simply and quickly in the workshop than on the site. Working conditions are more favourable; they are not subject to the weather, and if large numbers of prefabricated dwellings are required, machine production has a great advantage in that most of the work can be done in the same place. Here then the introduction of machine production in MH has its great chance. This attraction, however, is at the same time the weak spot in attempts at prefabrication, undertaken so often in the past without any striking success. What exactly happens? A number of MH dwellings or blocks are designed, intended for realisation by the machine and prefabrication. But to do this with any chance of financial success, it is essential, as in all mass production, that the factory works uninterruptedly and produces a continuous stream of these dwellings in large numbers. Seen in terms of housing this is the purest and most unadulterated form of MH one can think of. It is in fact precisely what Van der Waerden imagined, and we have tried to show at some length why this solution, ostensibly so obvious, is doomed to failure.

Again we encounter the questionable idea that the machine and MH are insolubly connected. Now machine production does presuppose prefabrication, for this production consists after all of manufacturing parts in a factory, before their assembly as complete dwellings. The point is that these need not be MH dwellings because the machine is not concerned with the uniform dwelling.

If machine production did not exist, MH would indeed be the only method in which prefabrication makes any sense. In that case, work carried out in the workshop would be similar to that on the building site, excepting its production under better conditions. It would then be reasonable to build a certain number of dwellings again and again (by prefabrication) just as that was reasonable in the emergency situation of the pre-machine age. But it makes no sense to keep thinking in terms of such a situation: *the point is that it is precisely the machine which liberates prefabrication from the slavery of* MH, *and makes prefabrication without* MH *possible.* To arrive at this we must forget the fatal question of how to make MH effective, and return to the vision of a housing process in which, next to the natural relationship, the machine also has a part to play.

A trusted relationship

It will now be possible to take a closer look at the play of forces which will engender the housing process of the future, for, taking as our starting point a fully-mechanised production system, the natural relationship is now recognised as a genuinely essential factor. Mechanisation will have to concentrate on the continuous production of groups of elements, which need not result in uniform dwellings, but can be assembled in an endless variety. Let us for a moment think of the production of the modern kitchen. We see how different manufacturers market kitchens consisting of elements which, by means of dimensional standardisation, can be fitted together in innumerable variations. There are sink units of different lengths and widths, different cupboards which can be placed beside or above them, systems which allow the inclusion of dishwashers, cookers, washing machines, refrigerators; the principle is as wide and complete as one may wish. A similar idea has been applied with success to the furniture industry by marketing storage units in various dimensions which may be assembled and re-assembled in numerous combinations. In this way, the user can realise his wishes according to his own choice and buying power, and because the number of variations is inexhaustible, industry can afford the research and investment necessary for the effective production of a limited group of elements. Industry can thus hope to find an outlet for these elements throughout the country without damage to the spontaneous variety of life.

Such a method can only work when the potential of variation is exploited, and the catalyst of variation is the consumer. Industry therefore prefers to deal directly with the consumer, and to a large extent needs his reactions and active interest to achieve an effective product. Thus it turns to market research and aims constantly at what is simpler and fits better within a given price scale. A direct interplay between consumer and producer is therefore apparent. When we reach the point at which component production can be undertaken for assembly into dwellings, the natural relationship will inevitably enter into the sphere of the housing process. With that, an age-old relationship will be restored. None of the existing forces in the housing process would be eliminated: architects, town planners, building contractors, technicians and experts in every field, would relate to each other in such a way that the process would constantly and naturally improve.

The independent dwelling

Although the manufacture of such products in such an industrial system would undoubtedly facilitate the restoration of the natural relationship, it would be a mistake to assume that this restoration would result automatically. To ensure this we should not take a production system as our starting point. In the first place, it is by no means certain that we can at once organise industry in this way, and expect it to work effectively. Secondly, it is questionable whether dwellings thus produced would be economically justifiable, for, however proud we may be of our technological power, industrial production in this respect results rather in an improvement in quality than in a decrease in cost. Whatever the case, for the time being we can regard the possibility so far outlined only *as possibility* and not as a means of introducing the natural relationship. Our problem was, and remains, of a non-technical nature.

We should not try, therefore, to reach a technical ideal but, by establishing the right balance of forces, create the conditions for working towards this goal. This can only happen if we turn our backs on MH. And there is another important condition which we have not yet considered.

In a relationship there are always at least two interacting factors. In the case of the natural relationship they are the dweller and the dwelling. We know as yet nothing about the latter, for we have purposely avoided imagining it. Without actually doing so we may nonetheless ask ourselves whether there is a dominating quality which will characterise for us this partner in the natural relationship.

MH proved indifferent to the natural relationship because as soon as it had to deal with a project involving several people, the activity of the individual occupant was prevented. A relationship cannot come about if one of the participants is immobilised. To enable the natural relationship to function a dwelling should be capable of being altered, remodelled, pulled down and rebuilt without affecting any other dwelling. The dwelling in the natural relationship is an independent dwelling.

This does not mean, it should be said at once, that our independent dwelling is necessarily a freestanding one. Certainly a detached house is independent, but it is superfluous to demonstrate that in our society the entire population cannot live in detached houses! It has long been necessary to build high and this necessity may well have been responsible for the gradual disappearance of the natural relationship. It means, therefore, that before we can reintroduce the natural relationship we must find a way to build independent dwellings on top of each other.

Only thus can we make use of the social and technical possibilities which have been outlined.

When, through lack of space or the need to build compactly, the dwelling is lifted off the ground we are faced with 'lumping together dwellings into one large project'—from which MH arose. It might even be said that in leaving the ground man left the natural relationship behind. There is no way back: we cannot return to ground level. This may be the reason for Holland's apparently insoluble housing shortage. For, to take a different case, in America where there is plenty of ground, and greater distances are overcome by the motor car, the MH disaster has until now been largely prevented by the monstrous expansion of the suburb. In this connection it is interesting to note that the moment circumstances became similar to those in the Netherlands, the same problems made their appearance. What is called 'social housing' there, the large-scale housing of slum dwellers in enormous blocks of flats, exhibits to such an extent all the repellent consequences of total MH that any such attempt is thought to be doomed to miserable failure.

But this approach means that no other course is open than the depopulation of cities and the growth of suburbs, so that town centres remain only business centres or become slums— a problem which grows increasingly acute. In the Netherlands, therefore, we are forced to come to terms with it. This country is over-populated: we must build high and compactly. At the same time, our living standard is high, higher even than in the wealthy US where conditions are found in black and working districts which would be unthinkable here. Our task therefore is primarily to find a solution to the great problem of society: *to find a formula for a housing process which allows comfort and human dignity to exist hand-in-hand, while maintaining the town as conglomerates of compact building*. The problems which confront us will manifest themselves inevitably in one form or another in every civilised country where living standards rise but space is at a premium.

To arrive at a contemporary housing process several questions must be answered. How are we to build so that each dwelling achieves the independence necessary to make it a fully-fledged partner in the natural relationship? And how is this to happen without going back to putting everything at ground level? This may be put in another way. If we consider the town, and in particular the town centre, as a conglomerate of buildings, we may say that each building is independent in the sense described above, and that it may be erected or pulled down independently of other buildings. The necessity to build high makes buildings larger, thus getting further away from the situation when each dwelling was an independent building. In the organism of the town we may see the independent building as a cell leading its own life, rejuvenating and renewing itself in response to impulses from society. The ideal of the natural relationship requires these cells to be small and to correspond to the cells out of which society itself is constituted. Only in this way can a maximum of harmony exist between man and matter as time progresses. The necessity of making towns out of larger blocks causes a coarsening of the town structure. The extent of the town may increase enormously, but the number of cells it contains becomes less. The new quarters of Amsterdam contain more inhabitants than the old but they are built up from a far smaller number of cells. These districts are not large towns, but enlargements of small towns; villages seen through a magnifying glass. When we regard the image of the town as an organism built up from living cells, it becomes clear that our new towns are primitive organisms with a coarse, inflexible structure capable of little life, albeit on an unnaturally large scale.

In a really modern town one would have expected an infinitely complex and refined structure, composed of far more cells than the old town. This organism would thus be a unique phenomenon, the cells forming organs and groupings appropriate to a very large town, just as in nature highly complicated beings develop more than one organ.

The large, but structurally extremely primitive, towns we build now are in total conflict with a society which is developing into an increasingly complex entity with more and more organs, *all, however, composed of the same cells as those in the past!*

The demand that the natural relationship be reintroduced is nothing but an inevitable desire to make town structure conform to that of society; the desire to reach in a metropolis the structural harmony between matter and population found only in smaller towns of the past.

Historically, it would be interesting to trace the social and cultural consequences of this inability to build large, finely-structured towns: how in the end one had to find refuge in an increase of scale and coarsening of structure which now appears disastrous to us, and which was always connected with the masses and the proletariat. I believe that such an investigation into the 'biology of towns' would give us a far better insight into these intractable phenomena that affect our life. But we cannot await the creation of such a new science and must try now to create conditions for future towns which, because of their great size, must be made up of small cells.

The growth of an urban organism depends entirely upon the techniques mastered by its inhabitants. It would not be possible, for example, to build a town of any extent without a reasonable sewage system. Without it a degree of uncleanliness would develop which, even if the population did not succumb to disease, would simply silt up the place. Small towns or villages could exist without a sewage system by relying on a nearby stream or external refuse dump. But as towns grow larger sewage systems become a condition of existence. The organism requires a new organ for its continued growth. In the same way, roads, electricity, gas, water, telephones and public transport are so many new organs which make life possible in a modern town. Experiments are even carried out in public heating systems, not for our increased convenience but because pollution caused by individual heating has superseded bad drainage as a major threat to public health.

The invention of the safety lift is another typical example. It is not accidental that this took place in Chicago, at the very moment when the city underwent a period of enormous growth, and the need to build upwards made itself felt. Together with the steel frame, which began to replace heavy monolithic construction, it made possible the birth of the skyscraper, and within the space of a few years, dozens of these hitherto unknown structures appeared in a street a few miles long.

The flashpoint of our town-planning development is now unquestionably in the field of housing. The coarsening of town structure and the discrepancy between town and society has reached intolerable proportions. The technical task which faces us is therefore not the prefabrication of MH, nor its mechanisation, but this: we must arrive at the independent dwelling and the associated restoration of the natural relationship, so that the town will acquire a natural structure where what is small should be small, and what is large can be large.

Towards a housing process

Gradually, it appears to me, the essence of the housing problem has emerged. *It should be possible to discover a method in which man and machine, natural relationship and mass production, are given full opportunity to unfold side by side.* The conflict between these two quantities exists only in MH.

Even if only by way of opening the discussion, I intend to sketch out such a method in the following pages. I mean to remain faithful to our starting point: to seek a full realisation of our housing task. This of course includes the relationship of forces which can be balanced when MH is abandoned; the relationship between society and town, the development of modern technology as the inspiring impulse for daily life.

Relationship of forces thus remains our subject. The relationship between man, matter and machine is still our main preoccupation. But to enable this relationship to function we need a plan, however summary it may be. Because examples are wanting we have to conjure up an image of the contemporary town, a town, that is, which is feasible today and in which all these relationships are in operation. Thus we cannot avoid thinking as form givers, *but only in the sense that we must find a solution in principle* which will contain that balance of forces which we consider essential.

This is a different matter from *producing a design*. The visual aspects of the formal proposals appearing in subsequent pages are therefore *not* to be regarded as sketches for a design. They are forms resulting from a new working method as I see it. It is the *method* which is important. Whether the forms are pleasing or not will depend on those who apply the method. That is a matter of design.

The question asked here is whether the method will open up prospectives and possibilities so painfully absent until now.

If we agree about a force-relationship which will enable us to build more productively, which will bring together town and society, and which will allow the natural relationship to come into its own the forms will emerge almost by themselves. They will appear from all sides by the inventiveness and intelligence of all those concerned.

Therefore what I think as architect, as formgiver, is of interest only in so far as it illustrates that a new relationship of forces is not only needed but possible. However much I may be convinced of the viability of the forms I see arising out of the ruins of MH, their role in this respect is secondary.

The creation of a town is first and foremost the outcome of a thought process. It would be an empty gesture, therefore, if I were to rush in with a design for the town of the future (even if I had such a design) before agreement had been reached as to the way in which this process works. Only then could drawings, as suggestions for the results of the process, have any value.

There is, therefore, no sense in asking what I would want, or in demanding drawings, forms, designs, concrete plans. What I want is not very important, for we may be sure of one thing: whatever the future brings, it is bound to be different from what I now imagine.

But it *is* important to concern ourselves with the *manner* in which the town of the future will come about, and with its essential conditions.

THE SUPPORT STRUCTURES

To allow the development of natural relationships in the urban situation we must, as we saw before, regard each dwelling as an independent one.

The first and greatest difficulty we encounter when we wish to envisage a town consisting of independent dwellings, is the necessity to place these dwellings on top of each other. Simple lack of space precludes the possibility of building them side by side the only independent dwelling we know, now as in the past, is the detached house.

The first requirement, to build upwards, is at once the care and the glory of town-planning activity. To pile dwellings on top of each other has always meant that several of them constitute one building. It is the first step towards that dangerous increase of scale which threatens living conditions and the subtleties of town organisation. On the other hand, the need to build high can lead to the creation of genuine towns of life and character by means of outline, mass and open spaces.

How can the latter possibility be maintained whilst avoiding the dangers of мн? How do we pile up dwellings without sacrificing their independence? This is the great problem of design and technique which requires a solution.

The answer can be simple and comprehensive. We must make constructions which are not in themselves dwellings or even buildings, but are capable of lifting dwellings above the ground; constructions which contain individual dwellings as a bookcase contains books, which can be removed and replaced separately; constructions which take over the task of the ground, which provide building ground up in the air, and are permanent like streets. Without for the moment considering their appearance, I would name these constructions support structures, after their function. Every construction, therefore, enabling us to build independent dwellings which do not stand on the ground, is a support structure. I propose this definition: *A support structure is a construction which allows the provision of dwellings which can be built, altered and taken down, independently of the others.*

Although this proposal seems inconceivable at present, it will be shown to offer us unsuspected possibilities. On the one hand support structures restore the natural relationship, on the other they allow full exploitation of modern factory-based mass production. They overcome, therefore, the two principal shortcomings of MH which were revealed in the previous chapters.

Intermezzo

A married couple want to settle down in a support-structure town. They find a space in a structure where they can assemble their dwelling. In *this particular* structure the space is as follows. The support structure consists of a concrete construction of a number of floors one above the other, stretching out through the town. Between these floors are the dwellings, side by side. A zone at one side remains free as a walking gallery which connects freestanding staircases and lift shafts, placed at regular intervals. Between two floors there is an open space, until recently taken up by a dwelling but now removed. This space is limited top and bottom by the support floors, and to left and right by the blind walls of the other dwellings. On the gallery side there is nothing, nor on the opposite side: openings which presently will be filled in.

This space suits our couple for various reasons. They decide to have a dwelling constructed there. To this end they study information, trade literature and different manufacturers' displays of support structure dwellings. After much thought, they make up their minds, and visit the showrooms of the manufacturer of their choice. With the help of a representative of the firm an effective arrangement of a dwelling is decided upon. Because support structures have long since become common property and their housing technique perfected, the dwelling in question can be totally formed out of prefabricated elements.

The representative invites our customers to return in a fortnight. The dwelling will then be ready for inspection in the showrooms. At the appointed time, they see a full-scale model of their dwelling. They walk about in it, test doors and windows, visit kitchen and bathroom, try the usefulness of rooms and cupboards. After suggesting a few alterations they decide to buy. The manufacturer transports the parts to the support structure where the dwelling is finally assembled in a short time. The local authorities connect gas, water, electricity and drainage to supplies under the approach gallery and the buyers can move into their new home.

Further description of the function of support structures

Although certain forms of support structures present themselves almost automatically, we obviously cannot at this stage come to any conclusion about their *exact* form. For the moment, we are concerned with the play of forces which engenders cities and by means of which they exist. The supports in this respect are of importance only in so far as they constitute a condition by which this play can function within our present condition and in conformity with our requirements. We should, therefore, approach these structures not via their forms but via their function. When their function has become clear, their form will soon develop.

How will the forces we met act upon the support structures? What is the housing process which will develop from them? These are questions which now demand our attention.

It is important that we do not allow ourselves to be influenced by forms and constructions with which we are familiar. I am not suggesting, however, that such forms cannot teach us anything, nor that we shall not need the knowledge and skills implied in these constructions. But today's forms are associated with functions which we want to replace, and the danger is that this association, if we are not conscious of it, may prevent us from recognising the unique functions of support structures.

A support structure is quite a different matter from the skeleton construction of a large building, although to the superficial spectator there may appear to be similarities. The skeleton is entirely tied to the single project of which it forms part. It can be realised only when the new building, and all that is connected with it, has been worked out in detail. A support structure, on the other hand, is built in the knowledge that we cannot predict what is going to happen to it. The more variety housing can assume in the support structure, the better. It is therefore not an uncompleted building, but in itself a wholly complete one.

Although in designing a support structure we certainly have to keep in mind what is to happen there, its design and building are quite different from those of the dwellings. Similarly, street layout differs from the construction of the buildings alongside it, although there is the strongest connection between the two.

As the future content of the support structure can be known

only in very general terms, its form and construction must be of the utmost simplicity; all the more so because it is to be constructed on the site. In contrast to the dwellings, it should not have the complicated detailing, nor the precise finish, nor the short-term existence of the factory product. It is brute construction, of the same order as bridges, viaducts, canals or roads: works which have a close connection with the earth and are erected relatively slowly and with difficulty, in all weathers. Works, also, which withstand the centuries: the more robust, the more they repay the trouble of their construction.

In considering support structures we must distinguish between building in the traditional sense and exploiting to the full the potential of the factory product. By separating these two methods and giving them their own range each can attain its full development. The perplexing conflict encountered in MH between building technique and factory production has thus disappeared: the first triumph brought about by reintroducing the natural relationship.

Support structures therefore have a rational basis, and rest upon a clear appreciation of how the machine is to be introduced into housing. Machine production is not over-estimated, but it is given the opportunity to act according to its nature. Thus the support structure is a functional solution to the novel problem of our era.

But we should do an injustice to our problem (which concerns every aspect of human habitation) if this one advantage satisfied us. The support structure is not merely the functional solution of a technical problem: it orders, by means of the natural relationship, the entire system of housing dynamics.

The support structure will leave no facet of contemporary housing untouched: the whole field of modern architecture will be affected by it, and industry will have to adapt to a new building approach, which in extent and production capacity will exceed the motor car industry. In short, the principle of support structures will inaugurate a new age in building and living.

In considering MH we saw how the general acceptance of this method was the cause of a desperate shortage. As the reason for this shortage was not recognised it was difficult to gain an insight into the situation in which we were landed. When something goes wrong the natural reaction is to look for a disturbing factor which may be *removed*. In the case of our housing it turns out that something has to be added!

Support structures then become as it were the symbol of

what is missing; they restore the natural relationship and their influence will be felt in the furthest fibres of the town's organism.

All the same, we cannot expect that concrete armadas will suddenly disappear from the fields and that new forms will shoot up. Our first task will be to fully understand the new force-relationships, and to see that the situation in industry, on the building site, in architecture and government is reviewed in this perspective. In the following pages, when searching for a new equilibrium, we must take care not to fall unconsciously into the error of setting up relationships and criteria which we have just rejected: a well-known danger which frequently threatens this field of enquiry.

Industrial possibilities of support structures

In speaking of support structures and their dwellings we must clearly differentiate between the fully-developed situation in which the new relationships function properly and the transition period during which the new organism moves through various stages of growth. The most spectacular developments are to be expected in the industrial field.

Housing—as distinct from support structures—will be the offspring of modern production techniques. Here the idea of assembling prefabricated elements can be fully worked out. Technically it will be possible to assemble a dwelling like a box of building blocks, and the extent to which this can be carried is largely determined by economic factors. As human labour becomes more expensive it will make sense to employ the machine, and limit labour on the site to simple assemblage.

To this end, large enterprises entirely devoted to the manufacture of prefabricated dwellings will be required. In their mass production, research, development and extent of markets they will be comparable to the motor industry. Where they differ greatly from this example, however, is that the variations required in housing will lead to the manufacture of groups of elements from which innumerable dwelling types can be made up. Such groups may be, for example, external wall elements, internal partition elements, floor elements, storage elements, doors, kitchen elements, bathroom elements, etc. All these groups will have different price ranges, and therefore differ in quality, finish and design. Within each group an infinite variety of combinations is possible. An industry will therefore arise which will market various groups of elements competitively. The trade names of these groups will attain a conceptual power comparable to those of motor cars: concepts which will denote a certain style or quality, efficiency or detailing.

Many aspects of the relationship between product and buyer, as we know it in the sale of industrial products, will also relate to housing. The producer will maintain constant contact with the public by means of his sales organisation. It will therefore be in his interest to be fully aware of the wishes and requirements of his customers, and to try to express these requirements as fully as possible in the finish, quality and price of his product.

After-sales contact would also be in the interest of both producer and consumer. The manufacturer could institute an after-sales service in the way it is now done with washing machines, refrigerators and motor cars. Such a service would be advantageous to the consumer, for his possession would receive expert maintenance whilst he enjoyed the maximum return for his outlay. Similarly, the producer would be given the opportunity to keep himself informed of the behaviour of his products in daily use. This would increase his chance both of selling further components and undertaking eventual alterations.

The opportunity for change or renewal of the dwelling leads to an interesting speculation. It is obvious that with support dwellings an industrial law will operate which allows the durability of the product to be determined by use. It would not be difficult, of course, to manufacture dwellings which are practically indestructible, but it is reasonable to expect that support dwellings, in contrast to the sort of dwellings we have known until now, will have a comparatively short life.

Industry will no doubt market new series of elements from time to time, which, if not better, will at least differ from their predecessors in design and detail. The frequency with which these series succeed one another will probably be slower than, to use the comparison again, those of the motor industry. I do not believe that industry can force the public to buy new products constantly. It would ultimately lead to consumer revolt. A balance will be determined by usage and will change according to time and place. Perhaps the average couple will purchase a totally new dwelling. Perhaps the dwelling will be so expensive that at first a second-hand one is acquired, and a new one assembled later on. Perhaps a dwelling can be hired from a manufacturer, and later, when a family has reached its full extent, it will move into its own. Among the better situated it may become customary to change one's dwelling according to one's changing condition: from married couple to family with small children, with older children, with studying children, to old couple. Some people will doubtless consider it due to their wealth or position to house themselves in the very latest designs, and collectors may try to conserve a dwelling assembled from a vintage series no longer available. Who shall say?

The most important thing in this respect is that the support dwelling offers an endless range of possibilities. Housing will have its Cadillac as well as its Volkswagen, its Bentley and its *deux-chevaux*. But there is one most important difference: a dwelling is no motor car and no dwelling need be the same as any other. The motor car allows us to perform a single act: we move from place to place. But a dwelling contains at least one whole life.

Moreover the dwellings will have to be assembled on the site which in itself affords an opportunity for variation. A comparison with the modern kitchen is therefore more apt than with a car. There, on a small scale, is an illustration of the principle which allows great variety of execution and arrangement by means of industrially-produced elements. Every housewife wants her sink, cooker, refrigerator, cupboards and shelves in a different place from her neighbour, although in all these variations a similar pattern may be discerned. A similar differentiation will always occur in the dwelling, even though every country, every generation, will demonstrate a certain unity. The variety which becomes available and which is of incalculable value to society will show itself especially in minor matters. The instinctive idiosyncrasies of the average person are, in this respect, of far greater importance than the deliberate originality of an individual. The richness of daily life shows itself, after all, in the adaptation of innumerable trifles to personal existence: the placing of a certain window or door, a light switch or storage space, the combination of different spaces or the privacy of a separate room. All these relatively unimportant matters, without which a man would doubtless continue to live, are yet, as we saw, of great consequence. It was because of this that it became necessary to oppose MH, the indifference of which brushed these matters aside.

Support dwelling is essential if the evolution of living itself is to take place without hindrance. As a housing form it caters for unexpected, rapid changes in current opinion. Experimenting with a life style can take place only when we are freed from the fear that presently we shall be landed with dwellings representing opinions which meanwhile have become obsolete.

It enables matter to follow man more readily than ever.

Through direct contact with consumers and the collective experience possible only in large-scale enterprises, we can begin to aim purposefully at what is better and simpler. The reaction of inhabitants to what is offered them will be the continuing stimulant necessary for healthy development. An unsatisfactory detail will not remain on the market if a better one may be obtained elsewhere, as this would represent an immediately-felt financial loss to the producer. The building industry will therefore respond closely to the voice of the inhabitant. Here we see the natural relationship in action as an influential factor in the production of housing.

It is difficult to gauge the acceleration of the industrial development of building which could occur if support housing is accepted. When we remember the fabulous revolution which took place, for example, in transport throughout the first half of this century, we may form some conception of what may be accomplished in housing during the second half. The support-housing industry will have the added advantage of a ready-made mass-production apparatus at its disposal. An enormous reservoir of technical know-how is ready to be tapped and full use can be made of experience gained in other fields. Attention can thus be focused on the product itself and not on the development of new methods of production.

Because for the first time in history great industries will devote themselves to the construction of dwellings, it will not only be possible but essential that these enterprises set up research departments. Here at last, responsible scientific and technological investigation can be undertaken to arrive at better design and execution of the elements of a dwelling. Extensive and continuous tests can be carried out on windows, doors, conduits, insulation materials and innumerable small details upon which the effectiveness of the dwelling depends. All this can be done with the best and most costly equipment available and its results will exercise an influence far beyond the confines of housing itself.

The image which is conjured up is that of a building industry which has at last shaken off the bonds of tradition and attained maturity. As will appear later on, none of the suggestions made here are new or original but, as a result of the support structure idea, all the factors demanded for so long have suddenly assumed the surprising stature of a reality lying within our reach and an entire range of requirements at once fall into a logical pattern. We might even say that in dealing one by one with the consequences of support structures, we are engaged in the ordering of a larger number of potentials which, by rest-less labour of mind and body in other fields, have piled up against the barrier of MH. Now that this barrier has been broken, they can with confidence be ranged in a sensible relationship. Later, when we have completed our tour of the support town we shall be able to see this ordering activity as a whole. In the meantime, however, there is much to be discussed.

The form of support structures

Support structures stand outside the industrial field which produces support dwellings. Their function, after all, is to isolate those portions of building activity which cannot be carried out in the factory. Their erection, therefore, will be somewhat slow and relatively costly. It will be difficult to lay down the number of working hours, and the work will be sub-ject to the whims of weather and temperature and the irregu-larities of the ground on which they are built. Even if it were only because of this, it would be sensible to destine the support structures for as long a life as possible. In contrast to the dwellings they contain, they should withstand the ages. Their age should be no drawback to the development of the support-dwelling technique, for their forms are intended to allow for the unexpected.

Nevertheless, it is also feasible to make use of tried modern techniques to render the construction of support structures efficient. In order to get some idea of this we must envisage a form of structure. I have already mentioned that there will doubtless be many forms and construction methods, and that it is not possible at this stage to determine which is the best. But to estimate the advantages they offer, it will be enough to take the simplest form which presents itself. In the following pages, therefore, we shall confine ourselves to an idea I have already mentioned: parallel planes running one above the other and carried on columns. This would be the most primitive form imaginable.

Of course, it would be worth speculating on other forms of support structures. I could, for instance, think of supports which would allow the inclusion of dwellings of more than one floor. Such structures are indeed feasible, but in discussing them we should be led down a road we must not follow until we have outlined more precisely the new relationships between man and matter which are our first concern. So back to the simple prototype.

When we ask ourselves how best to make such a structure, considering the special circumstances under which it is built, it seems obvious that here we can fully apply the principle of repetitive actions on which MH is based. I have already suggested that support structures are no more than building plots up in the air and that they are of the same nature as streets in the familiar town. In the construction of roads the repetitive principle is also followed. Groups of workmen and equipment are formed which operate in sequence. First a wide trench is dug in which a bed of sand is placed, and upon this are built the various services and layers of the road surface. Each phase is the work of one group. They move at short distances from each other across the landscape, leaving behind them a clear and flawless trail. The same system can be adopted in building on a site: the production apparatus moves, but the product stands still.

When we apply this method to the building of support structures, the manner in which the groups are composed will of course depend upon the exact nature of the structure. If, for example, it is of reinforced concrete placed *in situ*, it will be totally different from working in steel framing. But whatever the chosen construction there are two general conditions which must be fulfilled: the support structure must have, as far as possible, the same section at any given point, and it must be as long as possible.

The first requirement means that all vertical circulation should preferably be on the outside of the structure. The second suggests that support structures will produce long ribbon-like forms. Both conditions are entirely in accord with the nature of support-structure living, for if we try to achieve the greatest freedom of use, staircases and lift shafts would be obstacles when placed inside the structure. Similarly, there is no reason to make these structures short: the longer the floors, the easier it will be to partition them into different 'building plots'.

From this we can form a picture of support-structure ribbons stretching across the land in certain patterns, and flanked by towers containing stairs, lifts, drainage and services connected by walkways on the several floors. When we consider the town-planning aspects of support structures we will have an opportunity to look more closely into this image. For the moment, we are concerned with the fact that a rational construction method evidently suits the support-structure idea.

There is a further opportunity of introducing modern construction techniques in the support structure. Because of its great length and unvarying section, it should be possible to assemble it economically from prefabricated elements. I am thinking here, for instance, of factory-produced columns, beams and floor elements, etc.: large elements relying for transport and manipulation on cranes and lifting trucks, all of which would ensure speed of assemblage.

At this point we might ask who will be responsible for the building of support structures. It seems obvious to me that this work should be an integral part of all preparatory operations required for the realisation of new quarters of towns. Decisions about road patterns, drainage and public services will depend on what is known about the particular support structures they serve, and where they are positioned. Gas, water, electricity and drainage conduits will have to be carried *into* the structures to enable connections with single dwellings to be made. Whilst, therefore, the provision of support *dwellings* can remain in private hands, support *structures* themselves should be part of government or local authority investment; necessary, like roads and services, for the growth of neighbourhoods or towns. After all, support structures are building ground, and since the preparatory 'cultivation' of the earth's surface for building development is a public undertaking, building ground up in the air forms part of such an enterprise.

We may speak in this sense of the three-dimensional town. In comparison, the familiar new town with its sky-high buildings is no more three-dimensional than the medieval town. In the support city the town plan acquires an extra dimension. *A support structure is not the skeleton of a building, but all the dwellings together form the skeleton of a town; a framework for a living and complex organism.* This leads us to town-planning considerations of the support city.

Town planning and support structures

With the appearance of support structures as the framework for a city, we can at once draw a clear line between the activities of the town planner and the architect. The town planner can now get a firm grip on the matter. He can—to recall an earlier metaphor—cultivate his garden in such a way that conditions for the growth of a living culture are set up. Now he can do it in three dimensions: his field is no longer two-dimensional town design but the mass of the town itself. By designing support-structure ribbons in a certain pattern, he can organise the town as a network of mutually-related building planes and lay down scale and extent, determine closed spaces, outline green areas, give context to freestanding buildings, and reach conclusions about main lines of development. Moreover, all this can take place without violence to the accidentals of life, the influence of the inhabitants or variations in dwelling patterns. A town image is emerging which offers fascinating opportunities for form-giving, and will afford a formidable challenge to the greatest talents in design for living.

The whole idea of MH necessitated the freestanding block. From time to time architects have attempted to influence the resulting planning form by designing dwellings in long ribbon-like sequences. As these ribbons inevitably became in themselves large, individual MH blocks, such gestures provided no answer. Any gains in town-planning were minimised by the stronger emphasis on objections to MH. The long, flowing ribbon did indeed provide new spatial forms for the town, but at the same time, it created an endless wall of unrelieved uniformity. In addition, plans could not always be the same, thus raising the cost of such projects beyond reason. It proved that this type of MH block was too large and too complex, and, as a result, MH always fell back upon the rectangular block.

A demand for the avoidance of freestanding blocks can be explained in terms of city scale. To understand this we must be aware that we move about and experience the city at ground level. A great three-dimensional mass has a totally different effect from the two-dimensional 'street-wall' of an old town, which forms, as it were, a décor. The streets and squares, formed by such wall, are to our perception open spaces in which we find ourselves. Thus, when standing in a town, we ourselves are the centre: the town is organised *round us* and seems to address itself to us. This effect is of great importance in our walk about, and therefore in our relationship to the town. Above all, we feel protected: we may be standing in an open space, but we are not on the outside; we are *in the town*. This also allows us to orientate ourselves, because a town, built up as it is out of street walls, consists of a sequence of spaces: streets as long continuous spaces which, in their crossings, afford us orientation points, and squares and parks which form accents related to them. It is possible, therefore, that a town may be a vast sequence of constantly-changing perspectives, without causing us for a moment to feel spatially lost.

But when the walls are interrupted, and the city consists of a rhythmic organisation of great masses, we find ourselves in a totally different position. It is difficult to make spaces with which a pedestrian can relate. He no longer feels inside the town, but, on the contrary, has the impression that he has moved *outside* the buildings. He feels no relationship with spaces surrounding him, but sees himself pitted *against* enormous towering shapes. Housing blocks are spread over the fields like grazing cows, and the walker roams amongst a herd of gigantic creatures. The blocks, not man, threaten to become the centre of gravity. In professional terms, the spaces round the blocks are known as *residual space*.

It is possible, of course, to create an impression of closed and protective space by carefully siting the building blocks, and in town-planning circles there is a strong tendency in this direction. But there is no getting away from the fact that MH requires the free-standing block. It is the smallest independently-interchangeable unit of a town, and thus determines its scale. MH cities will always consist of freestanding blocks, because such an arrangement is entirely in accordance with the method which gave rise to it. For this reason, the town-planner cannot suddenly change over to long flowing ribbons of building if he wishes to create a different form of town or space.

This short diversion was necessary to show that the relation between the form of a city and its manner of building and housing, extends much further than might have been expected at first sight. For this reason, we must not expect to find the typical form of the MH town in a support town. We must not imagine the support town as a collection of frames: support structures will develop a town form entirely their own. By reason of their use and construction they would preferably be shaped as long ribbons and could, for example, give back to the town the quality of a sequence of characteristic spaces. In this way, the means to put man, and not the building, in the centre of the scene will be restored to us. Once again we can build the town round people, without in any way forcing the new forms into a straitjacket. The support town will, of course, have totally different spaces from the traditional one with its streets and squares, and no doubt it will take time for the new form to crystallise fully, but it says much for our new approach that it enables us to restore old and tested relationships between man and matter by wholly contemporary means.

All this confirms our image of the support system as a framework for the town. Without any doubt different systems will be proposed and it will be necessary to take regional and climatic conditions into account. It would be possible, for instance, to design a town consisting entirely of a network of support structures, with floors stretching throughout the town, dividing and crossing each other, and varying in number. Alternatively, support structures could be built in rings of relatively free forms (like an elastic band on a table top) and the town could consist of a number of such rings. Inside the

71

rings would be enclosed spaces where no fast traffic would be permitted, and thus the dwellings would overlook green spaces and trees. Heavy traffic with all its noise, smell and speed, could be arranged on the outside, or between concentric rings. Connections between the dwellings could be maintained by bridge passages at various levels.

Whatever the arrangement, the idea of a large number of related and connected support structures irresistibly presents itself. Another advantage involves one of the darlings of modern town-planning theory, which until now could not find practical application. For a long time, town planners have toyed with the possibility of circulation at different levels, and quite understandably: it makes good sense to separate slow traffic from the all-demanding motor car. The support-structure network will enable the pedestrian to wander untrammelled through the town. It will be his undisputed territory and the town will resume human scale. The walk-ways may be seen as streets, varying in width and occasionally occupying a whole floor. They could flow through the town criss-crossing it freely, and offer constantly changing views of spaces, other structure ribbons and buildings. Local circulation could take place above the busiest traffic, and separation between man and machine be effortlessly achieved.

Yet another architectural feature acquires a new meaning in this connection. The idea of raising a building on stilts, or pilotis, is not new, and has been frequently applied, but, however attractive the novelty, it makes little sense to raise a freestanding MH block above the ground. It is seldom necessary to drive underneath it when it can be by-passed, and by lifting a support-structure network on legs it can be made quite independent of the traffic: here again the three-dimensional town comes into its own. It would make perfect sense to run the traffic parallel with and *under* the support structures, so that the support pattern and the traffic network were identical. Thus, seen from the support structures, no busy roads would bisect the spaces and protected connections would exist throughout the town. It would be a simple matter to reach upper walkways from the covered roads by means of freestanding stairs or escalators.

Roof spaces would present similar opportunities. The flat roofs of large buildings have long exercised a great fascination for the architect. Furnished with gardens and provided with facilities for sport and play, cinema or theatre, they have been much talked about and even built. But the roofs of support networks are roads, boulevards or real gardens and their horizontal connections will increase their potential tenfold. We are no longer confronted with islands which are only accessible vertically, but an entirely new element in the urban landscape.

In considering these opportunities, we should remember that the time factor will play an important part, for we have been liberated from the static quality which characterises MH. *The support town does not have to be determined in advance: it can be cultivated.* The use of roof spaces and circulation on different levels may be accomplished in the course of the years. The town can always grow in its support structures for they can be raised or extended without detailed planning in advance: vertical connections may be added; horizontal connections replaced or removed. This factor, an ability to improvise upon the requirements of the moment, is of the utmost importance in assessing fully the value of support structures. Because support structures have a permanent character the town may change continually and yet remain the same. If, therefore, we consider the flexibility of the support network in conjunction with the opportunities for design and fulfilment, and remember that within the structures there is to be found an endless variety of dwellings— dwellings which will constantly renew themselves owing to an industrial apparatus—one invaluable fact emerges: *the support town will never contain slums; no redevelopment will be necessary; no part of it need ever be obsolete.* The dwellings may show differences in quality and finish according to their price range, one dwelling may be larger and more luxurious than another, but the age of the dwellings can be the same for all population groups. Social discrimination, in this respect at least, will be abolished.

Sociological aspects

Here we touch upon a serious criticism of MH. It was seen that the static character of this method implied that the population was constantly forced to migrate. Not only did the inhabitants have to leave a district before redevelopment was possible, but moving house was the only way of changing or improving one's living conditions. This objection does not exist in the support town. Here population movement will take place only as the result of sociological pressures or impulses, and people will find their dwellings according to their place of work or the kind of community they wish to be part of. Of course, it cannot be predicted in which direction the culture of a community will develop, but it is no longer of vital importance whether we know this or not. Whatever happens, wherever the social groupings of the future establish themselves, or whatever form they assume, it will all be possible without abandoning the principles upon which the town plan is based. Support structures fulfil the most important condition of town planning: *that the unforeseen can be absorbed.*

MH makes it virtually impossible for new districts to develop a clearly recognisable character. It is no accident that the most colourful districts in our large cities are to be found in the most dilapidated, ripe-for-redevelopment areas. More time is required for the growth of a community than MH takes to become obsolete, but growth should now be possible within dwellings which are kept up-to-date. The sociological implications of this justify a separate study, but even the superficial glimpse to which we are limited, shows how support-structure inhabitants can make their own impression on an area. They will choose their own make of dwelling elements and they themselves will be involved in the way these are made up. By their choice of dwellings and the way they are used, a community of inhabitants will be recognisable to an outsider. Moreover, the way in which a support structure is filled, the way in which the possibilities of circulation are exploited, the development of the roof and its various additions, will also betray something of the character of a community.

Thus, the proper functioning of the natural relationship not only allows the dweller to *possess* his dwelling in the fullest sense of the word, but similarly it allows inhabitants to possess their neighbourhood. In the course of time the use they make of the many variations and trifling changes offered by support structures, should cause clearly discernible differences in atmosphere and character from one part of town to another.

Of course there is more to a neighbourhood than dwellings: there are shops, schools, businesses, garages and a church as well. In MH it is important that a space is set aside in the design for all these things. As problems arising from this have been pointed out before, we need not go into them any further. When we see the continuous evolution of old town centres— how shops change, how work places establish themselves and disappear again—the rigidity of MH becomes evident. In MH everything must have its predetermined, unchanging place. But support structures need not merely contain dwellings, for a small shop could be accommodated and a tobacconist, a doctor, a solicitor, a day nursery, a community centre, sub-post office could all establish themselves. In each case the necessary space can be organised from the same elements which make up the dwellings, and in accordance with its requirements. Time and custom will suggest how far this is desirable, but the fact that experience can be gained and put into practice is of great value.

We have come a long way from the brick-and-mortar statistics which we found so disquieting. If the notion of integration is applicable anywhere, it is here. Who shall predict what it all will look like? How will future generations express the perfect industrial product within the reliable protection of ageing support structures? How will towns develop towards that finely-balanced relationship between support structures, trees, roads and water, which may ultimately equal our magnificent canals in their harmony and timelessness? How will man and matter grow together towards complete identity? We need no longer discuss whether 'the inhabitant' will want lots of glass in his exterior wall, or would rather admit less sun or light; whether 'people' prefer living-kitchens to living-dining rooms, whether children need bedrooms in which they can study or whether they will do their homework in the living room. The experience gained from the interplay between occupants and industry will show the way from case to case. Instead of theorising about 'the dwelling' we shall, by setting up game-rules for the use and subdivision of support structures, take part in a powerful movement towards new social relations, new dwelling forms, new cities.

Buildings other than support structures

What influence will support structures exercise upon the siting and construction of other buildings in the city? Though we can be sure that much will take place within the support structures, we can be equally certain that they alone will not make a town. Clearly it would be advantageous to make use of the enormous support-structure industry, its construction principles and the elements and products which it will have worked out.

It may have occurred to the reader that there is some similarity between the idea of large floor areas, in which spaces are formed by means of prefabricated elements, and the modern office building. This building is nothing but a large number of floors connected by stairs and lifts and protected by external walls hung from the structural frame—the so-called curtain wall. By means of movable partitions, the internal division of the work spaces can be altered in a single night.

But the office building also differs from the support structure filled with dwellings. It is a self-contained building, the skeleton of which is adapted to the requirements of the activity within. It has uniform external walls which are built as one unit and which will permit no incidental changes. The vertical circulation is entirely absorbed within the construction and the whole building is heated and ventilated by expensive, centrally regulated equipment.

All the same, it seems reasonable that office buildings should make use of internal and external wall elements designed and produced by the support dwelling industry, for the industry is entirely suited to this sort of work, and has at its disposal both the equipment and experience to carry out such special commissions quickly and efficiently. Perhaps the skeleton itself could make use of prefabricated elements designed for support structures and this could have economic advantages for certain projects. A third possibility is that smaller firms could indeed establish themselves in part of a support structure.

There are then, several intermediate stages between support structures and specialised buildings and it seems obvious to me that many smaller and larger independent buildings could make use of the support industry. The industry will own several patents for insulating panels, for efficient windows and doors of various types, and for all kinds of complicated connections and details required in prefabrication. It would make little sense, therefore, to design all these things separately for a single building.

Thus, it should be quite feasible to design single, free-standing dwellings with the aid of available support-dwelling elements. It will be necessary, of course, even in these small projects, to be clear about separating the supporting construction from external and internal walls. This is a theme with which many architects have experimented. The American Eliot Noyes, for example, has built houses by forming a simply-constructed, thin-shell concrete dome and subdividing the interior space by non-supporting elements. Buckminster Fuller has also carried out experiments in this direction but, generally speaking, not much has been done beyond a number of specialised instances, for wall elements would need to be on the market before the economic advantages of this approach could be realised. What could be simpler than to make a floor and suspend a roof above it, the form and construction of which pleases both architect and client, and then to arrange the resulting space by means of existing elements? This is particularly important when one considers that the quality and construction of such elements could not be approached by separate design and manufacture.

In this way, the construction of many small buildings could be easily realised. I am thinking now of schools, community buildings, shopping centres and such like. By designing floors and roofs for their special use, it would be simple, quick and inexpensive to complete a building with existing products, thus deriving full advantage from the experience of the support-dwelling industry.

One could take a step further and have specially designed elements produced by the industry. In this way, one's own dimensional system could be maintained whilst fully exploiting detailing principles and simple methods of manufacture.

But what part can the support-dwelling industry play in buildings which, by their function and architectural significance, must be unique? I am thinking of churches, theatres, large multi-purpose halls, large workshops, factories, restaurants, sports complexes, laboratories and town halls: in short, all those buildings whose form and function are closely tied up with deep study and original conceptions; buildings in whose design new problems must be solved, and in which architectural talent should rise to its highest achievements.

Here also the new industry will be able to contribute significantly, for it will have research facilities at its disposal to support further developments in building techniques. Here tests can be made, models built and tested and experience exchanged, at a level which cannot be reached at present. Besides, in its constant search for improvements, the industry will doubtless come across constructions and solutions which may not be applicable in its normal activities, but which may be of the greatest importance in developing specialised buildings or techniques. Thus a fruitful interchange could develop between industry and the architect. The former will aid the architect in finding details and solutions for problems at a high level, whilst the inventiveness of the latter will stimulate industry and motivate experiments which otherwise would not be undertaken.

Is this not the most normal situation imaginable—in which the uniquely sublime arises from the normal and average, like a flower from a healthy plant? When we come to think of it, all architectural achievements of the past, the cathedrals and palaces of earlier generations, arose from an inconspicuous but lively building tradition. Numerous incidental experiences and solutions were always passed on in a continuous process until they accumulated in the realisation of an exceptional building. Similarly, all inventions leading to great achievements fell back into the fertile soil of the general tradition, so that an organic rotation arose.

Although this may seem obvious, MH presents a very different picture. The artificiality of this method does not give us any instances of fruitful influence upon exceptional architectural achievement. All the technical innovations we can point to in MH were introduced from the outside in accordance with the law that the artificial does not live a life of its own, but has to be kept in existence by external forces. There is no question of a stimulating interchange between MH and the rest of building activity. On the contrary, MH appears as ballast which must be carried. It is more like a reduction or abstract of what can be done in architecture and all experiments in the field have taken place outside it. Future growth or change can only be allowed for in rare projects where the natural relationship has scope to assert itself.

The introduction of support structures and their associated industry, therefore, would be of inestimable value in the building industry. However revolutionary this new organisation of force-relationships may seem in comparison with what is taking place around us, it is no more than the restoration of a normal situation in contemporary terms.

We have seen, therefore, how the specialised building, arrived at in this way, will have connections with housing. But its different form will stand out all the more and at this stage we can form some visual idea of it, even though the support structures themselves are only vaguely imagined. We have already seen how the long, mutually-connected support structures will become space-forming elements in the town plan, and how in spite of their great size—or rather because of it—they will enable man to feel surrounded and protected, and to be absorbed as part of an all-embracing pattern. The specialised building can be strongly projected against this neutral background, and will be clearly distinguishable from the support network. It could thus regain a significance which in the MH town it had lost. Is not everything in MH monumental? Every block of flats, by its size and siting, assumes an arrogant monumentality which becomes obsessive when it is repeated explicitly and endlessly. Monumentality is not necessarily a matter of size. A relatively small building can have a monumental effect when it is clearly outlined against a neutral background. This background is missing in MH and neutrality is lost in a repetition of definitive forms. We noticed it before: the exceptional has disappeared and the customary has become exceptional. In restoring normality in all its colourful variety, support structures will provide the background against which the unusual will come into its own. No doubt this will come about in a way we cannot yet foresee, but the potential is there and we have taken another step towards the natural situation.

The living city

We have now more or less completed our quick tour round the support city. Certain important questions remain, an examination of which would shed further light upon the new relationship of forces. Before doing that, however, I should like to take a bird's eye view of our city to see how this organism will behave with the passage of time.

The main characteristic of the support city is that it does not have to await its decay passively, but can constantly assume new shapes under the pressure of events. We have seen how support structures offer the opportunity to form open and closed spaces, to accompany wide streets and contain parks and areas from which traffic is excluded. We have formed an image of a city built up from enclosed areas such as these. These would be spaces surrounded by support structures of varying heights and containing some hundreds (or thousands) of dwellings, outside which the traffic may roar. We can thus envisage a city built up from such cells or 'support rings', which need not necessarily be circular. Between them the traffic may do its worst, and inside them the pedestrian determines the scale. In the spaces between the rings lies the big city with its noise and speed, its asphalt and its grim aspect, whereas inside the differing rings human dignity can rediscover itself in new relationships and develop its own community atmosphere. We can now envisage a support structure network determined by such rings which are connected with each other by bridges above ground level, to enable pedestrians to keep away from the traffic.

Such a city would be organically divided into smaller units which, by their form and function, will become independent, and grow into district neighbourhoods. These neighbourhoods will gradually respond to the whims of their inhabitants as succeeding generations leave their signs of habitation. Let us probe a little deeper into the life of our support city, and try to imagine how life can change from generation to generation.

79

If we wish to keep noisy activities out and direct our attention inwards, the support rings must have their walkways and staircases on the outside so that dwellings are orientated towards the inside. How large should an internal space be? The size of an average market square, or larger? In an even density of population, the size will of course depend upon the height of the support structures, so there must be some optimum which it is difficult to determine. We should avoid right angles in our buildings and maintain the principle of the flowing line. Not only does this produce a less aggressive, less monumental form, but a support structure without right angles can be filled more easily. On the outside, where the stairs and lifts are situated, there will be garages forming buffer zones between carriageways and walkways. Under the structure, which stands on legs, there is a pedestrian street completely shut off on the outside by the garages, possibly by shops, and by the entrances to stairs and lifts. On the other side, there is the green open space with paths where only pedestrians and cyclists are admitted. Shall we put a school in the middle of the green? Or a community building or meeting hall? Or shall we place them to one side, under the structure, and overlooking the park? On top of the support structure there will be a continous terrace, with some special buildings like a cinema, a sports hall or club facilities. We could extend a stair and lift hall for one support-structure segment to a few storeys above normal roof height, to contain small flats, or possibly very large ones taking up the best part of the floor area.

It would also be possible to place some of the special activities under the structure, sacrificing the covered street, but freeing the roof for garden layout. It could even contain private gardens or allotments to prevent people spoiling the public areas. What a sight such a town would present from the air, with gardens on all the roofs!

All these suggestions are intended to free our thoughts from their traditional patterns, but before losing ourselves in fantasies we must keep one overriding factor before us: *the ability of support structures to grow, develop and change with what goes on inside.* When the support rings are built and provided with stairs and lifts, their further development will depend on the life which develops in them. When the occupants have cars, garages will be built; if they have a lively community life, facilities will emerge for this inside the structure, or outside, above or below. If in years of prosperity the occupants wish to improve their structure they may lay out a fine garden on the roof, or a sports centre. Or they may decide to pave the covered street under the structure—*their* structure —in a more ornamental way, or cover the columns with marble or whatever! If they feel they live in a 'fashionable' support structure, they will see to it that their dwellings are assembled from a good make of elements. In short, out of all these activities, large and small, an environment will emerge where they will feel at home, where they belong.

After a few generations, the character of a support ring will no doubt change, just as in older towns neighbourhoods and environments change. Perhaps the park will become a playground or sports field, and earlier ornamentation will be removed to make room for shops or workshops, or possibly a school or cafe. The public garden on the roof may be divided into private gardens.

On the other hand, a decrease in population will result in a greater freedom to use the available room in a support structure. It may be decided to keep an entire floor open so that in the middle of the structure a promenade will appear with a pub, or some shops, perhaps a hairdresser and a tobacconist. A floor might be reserved for small offices, or the consulting rooms of doctors and solicitors, and on such a floor wider walkways might be projected. Perhaps the subdivisions could be rearranged to give some of the larger dwellings private open spaces. It is also likely that freestanding penthouse flats with their own gardens will appear on the roofs.

So much for future dreams. It would be interesting in this respect to speculate on how much say the occupants will have in the development of those parts of the city which are outside their dwellings. It cannot be said too often that a new relationship between citizens and authority could develop. The occupants' responsibility for their own dwellings will be echoed outside, for the total building activity converges upon the inhabitants. Their reactions will determine the short-term change in a support city: without them there is no starting point and no development is possible.

When responsibility for his city is returned to the citizen, the town will once again be representative of its people. By identifying with its town, a population leaves its mark upon it, for better or worse, and the mechanisation of the housing industry will not affect this in the slightest. Just as a motor car may express a certain personality, bestowed on it by a manufacturer in response to his customers' wishes, various dwelling products may have their own character. This means that a population will get the city it deserves and we would hardly expect to find a population without any sense of style in an aesthetically considered town. Irrevocably, the level of civilisation in a population may be read from its town. Vulgarity or nobility, ostentation or reserve, love of fine materials or dull respectability—if these are the general tendencies of a community they will be reflected in its housing. To ensure the creation of a fine city, its population must be educated in such matters and the passive consumption-mentality which MH incubates must be transformed into active interest.

I do not believe that this will be particularly difficult. The very application of support structures may be a sufficient stimulant. Perhaps the first result of it will be that an occupant, eager for his amenities and aware of his status, will soon become keenly appreciative of the quality of the products available to him.

This appreciation has been largely lost at present. People lose interest in matters they cannot influence. Besides, the technical level is so low, in comparison with what is available in other fields, that it would be unreasonable to expect any great interest. Not surprisingly, we find in daily conversations about cars a lively interchange of knowledge, expertise and experience, while discussions about housing are one long complaint. When the spark of interest and personal concern is lit, the most important condition for a growing housing culture has been fulfilled. It is in this light that we must regard the arbitrary selection of possibilities in support towns. All this and much more can take place, not by precise planning of the future city, but by the creation of new circumstances.

Costs and financing

Naturally the next question concerns cost. It is not hard to predict that many will immediately reject the idea on financial grounds.

I am not competent to deal with arguments of a financial nature, but some general observations can be made just the same. Perhaps it is questionable whether cost matters in this respect, for we have been moving in an area which precedes economic and financial strategy. In short, the question is not whether we can afford the support town, but whether we can afford to do without it.

We are concerned with the quality of life itself. If there was any question of choice, there would be some point in asking whether we can afford support structures or not, but this is not the case. If the maintenance of civilisation could be assured without support structures we should not build them and our entire housing policy would then become an expensive whim. But I have shown that the opposite is true and that MH is the ruinous system which demands great sacrifices from us. As long as MH is the only alternative, support structures cannot be rejected on financial grounds. We can only make comparison on an economic basis when alternative systems are suggested which also permit the natural relationship to function within a modern technological setting. The support system can only be questioned fundamentally in two ways: is it right to restore the natural relationship and can this be done by any other means?

It is as absurd to ask whether support structures are economically justified as it is to ask whether our telephone system, electricity supply or modern traffic systems are justified. The development of a civilisation makes its own conditions. If, when Bell made his first primitive telephone, someone had forecast the extensive cablings, conduits, exchanges and laboratories necessary for this world-encompassing communication system, many would have written the whole thing off as an absurd dream; an attractive but irresponsible toy. But human society needed this new organ to further its development: a growing communications system was essential and the telephone came. Once the possibility was there, it had to come, on pain of the stagnation and recession of civilisation.

If the independence of dwellings opens up new ways of production and restores to people a field of activity, responsibility and pride, the support structure will be accepted for that reason. The cost factor is immaterial here, because the system offers wider and much-needed opportunities and at last puts dwelling firmly within modern society. It need no longer be assured by artificial means.

Besides, it is by no means certain that support structures will demand greater material sacrifices from society than MH. The artificial maintenance of a system which requires an extreme effort of laws and regulations *against* the natural tendencies of society must be a costly matter, although the extent of the cost in sacrifices and frictions is difficult to express in figures. The care required on the part of the authorities and the frustrations in human relationships are also cost elements which cannot be estimated in terms of money. Although of real significance, none of these factors can be included with any accuracy in the comparative-cost equation of support structures and MH. There are other considerations, however, which might lead us to suspect that support structures could be more 'economic' than may be supposed at first sight.

In the first place, there is the fact that support structures will have a very long existence. The question is, therefore, how much the average cost of a support structure will be affected by the framework itself. Doubtless, they will require considerable investment, but, in the long run, they might well prove to be the cheapest way of building dwellings above the ground. In MH the cost of 'holding dwellings up' has to be paid for as often as the site is redeveloped, while support structures do not have this disadvantage. From the point of view of public authorities, the support town would seem to be an intelligent investment, for as long as such a town need not be extended, all that is required of a local authority is a yearly sum for maintenance. It will not be necessary to renovate the town several times. The subsidies which are now sunk in housing would be much better spent on support structures.

Though independent, the support dwelling must also be considerably cheaper than the freestanding house. It has no floor or roof, and may be built without hindering any other activities. But in estimating the cost of these dwellings and the influence it will have upon their realisation, two important new factors should be kept in mind: the opportunity for industrial development and prefabrication, and the new relation of occupant to product. These factors make it impossible to arrive at the kind of accurate data-based estimate which is used in MH operations.

I do not believe that prefabrication will enable us to build dwellings which will absorb a smaller proportion of our income than is now the case. To design an effective prefabrication system we shall have to make use of good materials and carefully worked-out, complicated details. What is saved in man-hours on the site, will be spent on materials and machines. The advantage of machine production does not lie, therefore, in an absolute lowering of costs, but in raising standards of quality and an acceleration in building speed.

Once industrialised, housing will know no bounds in its improvement of quality. Every detail can be perfected, as, for example, in trains and ships. Doubtless this will be costly, but once support structures become commonly accepted, industry will have an enormous market. The history of industrialisation has shown us it is wrong to assume that quality goods cannot be widely distributed. The ideal dwelling, full of technical devices and details, may be unattainable at present to the man in the street, but that is not to say that the support dwelling industry cannot make this into a standard dwelling. In fact it is easy to imagine: the idea is no more startling than Ford's announcement that he would put the motor car within the reach of the worker.

There is a second factor we must keep in mind. It is quite probable that people will be prepared to spend a larger proportion of income on their dwelling than is now customary. After all, at the moment they are not offered much for their money. I do not believe that the support dwelling must be cheaper than the MH dwelling for it to be accepted by the occupants. In any case, it will be cheaper than a freestanding bungalow built to one's own requirements, whilst the ideals incorporated in such a bungalow will to a large extent be found also in a support dwelling. When people find that they can expand their way of life, they will be willing to pay for it and it would be foolish to predict that what is offered to them will be too expensive and therefore economically unjustifiable. In that case, television would not be economically justified, but the question whether or not television is viable has long since been decided by the public. The economic factor only plays a part when it comes to choosing between different TV sets.

Support structures will introduce so many factors of a psychological nature, that it is impossible to predict the relationship of support dwelling to economy. At the same time, the opportunities opened up by the independent dwelling may make the possession of one's own dwelling appear much more attractive. It seems obvious that a support-dwelling industry will encourage the tendency towards private ownership. In this respect, there are many possibilities: all kinds of purchase, hire purchase, instalment plans and hire schemes. Perhaps industry itself will profitably engage in the hire of dwellings. Various arrangements can be thought of to enable people, by periodic payments, to have their own dwelling assembled and industry may even find it worth its while to finance the erection of support frameworks.

Whatever arrangements are adopted, the support idea makes possible all the relationships between builder, owner and occupier which we know in the freestanding house. Nor need we assume that support dwelling is concerned only with private housing: for private ownership is no longer essential to give the occupier an active role in the housing process.

Support dwellings free us from the MH form of private property which, as we saw, is merely a legal concept. Support dwelling does not determine the degree of private ownership, and therefore does not stand in the way of a tendency which manifests itself more and more. Whereas MH does not answer the need for truly 'full-blooded' possession in the psychological sense of the term and can offer it only in the legal sense, support dwelling also lends itself in this respect to a familiar and natural relationship in a new form.

The way in which the support system characteristically provides as many opportunities as possible for the development of different relationships may be confusing to those trained in MH thought processes.

If this characteristic appears strange to us, it is because our thoughts are still bound up with the unfortunate split between society and the city—a split which commands the MH designer to crystallise the form of society in matter, as if he were making a close copy. Thinking in these terms, one tends to associate a definite building form with a certain concept of society, and vice versa. As he built, the architect would actually create the kind of society he believed he saw around him.

All the questions which arose from this approach—should 'the dwelling' have a separate kitchen or a kitchen-dining room; should 'the building block' dwelling types be provided, should 'the kitchen' connect with a balcony or only 'the living room'?—need not be answered in advance in support dwelling. They will be answered, again and again, in the course of the housing process. It will be perfectly possible for a developer or speculator to build a support structure full of uniform dwellings to be let. If such a course of action is in accordance with the society of which it forms part, he will profit by his venture. If not, his 'mass housing project' will vanish. Support structures not only provide something different from MH, they provide more. Where MH presupposes a certain type of society, support housing refuses to pose its own peculiar community; where a MH town is imaginable without inhabitants, empty and deserted, perfect and brand new, the support town cannot be predicted because it will arise *together with its community*.

The MH dwelling is always a firmly outlined phenomenon and therefore it can be calculated financially. With support dwellings this is only possible when a society has taken form in it and with it, so that types and techniques may be distinguished afterwards. Support dwelling is a game which must be played to arrive at a result: MH is a military parade where all movements are worked out in advance to prevent chaos. The game of support dwelling may be played well or badly, expensively or cheaply, in great freedom or in even greater slavery, but first we must decide whether we want to play at all.

Beginning

How are the first support structures and their dwellings to be created? How is the new play of forces to be set up? Obviously at this point no complete answer can be given. To make a start one needs at least a design—if only to put it forward for discussion among the numerous authorities and interested parties—and such a design does not exist. We deliberately refrained from such a course until the whole idea became clearer.

To design the first support structure, a team of experts and technicians in collaboration with various local authorities will be required. Support structures are town planning rather than architecture, and as such they will be closely associated with all kinds of technical provisions and preparations, indispensable in the expansion of towns. Of course it would be possible to make test types or laboratory designs to become familiar with the new method, but even for this, intensive discussions among experts would be necessary. The first requirement, therefore, is a favourable climate for a concrete development: hence this book.

Even when firm designs have been produced, complete with working drawings and estimates, considerable difficulties will occur before they can be built. It is not technology, but man himself that is the weak link in the chain leading to support cities, and we need cherish no illusions about this fact. It takes more trouble to change opinions and methods, to make interested parties see the advantages, to disentangle civil service procedures and clear up misunderstandings, than to rebuild an entire town.

There are, however, two factors ranged on the side of the protagonists of support dwelling. In the first place, there is ever-increasing disillusionment with MH and, in the second, one must take into account the attitude of the inhabitants once it becomes clear that a better way is possible. People will adopt support structures when the total failure of MH can no longer be denied, and this will come about the sooner it is realised that the rejection of MH is not a step into a vacuum, but a step towards a constructive solution. The unmasking of

87

MH and the exposition of alternatives are first and connected steps. Again: hence this book.

When attention is ultimately directed to the realisation of support structures, it would be wise to exploit to the full their characteristic ability to grow and change. We need not await a fully-fledged support-dwelling industry which can deliver completely prefabricated dwellings. The support-structure system can be grafted on to the existing situation and, in growing, change this situation totally. The idea of prefabrication is not essential to support dwelling: it is only an attractive aspect of the system that it allows prefabrication to be applied fully. Nor is it necessary to establish fully-equipped factories with all the investment this implies. With only the traditional building industry at our disposal, concrete support structures could be erected to contain perfectly ordinary dwellings. Later, these dwellings could be replaced by more advanced ones, and while the support remains constant, the dwellings can keep pace with the evolution of the building industry. The industry could move gradually in the direction of complete industrialisation, unimpeded by the old-fashioned MH technique which, as we saw, is hostile to the machine.

Dwellings created in this way would undoubtedly be more expensive than the MH dwellings of today, but the advantages already seem to be numerous:

Money invested in support structures will be well spent: authorities will not have to rebuild them. Dwellings need no longer be uniform. The occupant can determine the quality of his dwelling according to his requirements and his means. The arrangement of dwelling types and family types can proceed freely: brick-and-mortar statistics need no longer be consulted. The addition and adaptation of small shops and separate spaces or areas for communal use will require no artificial planning, but may be included in direct response to requirements. The active interest of the occupants returns along with their own responsibility. The construction of dwellings can to a large extent take place independently of the weather. Technical experiments, as well as experiments in the field of dwelling, can be carried out incidentally.

In short, a start can be made on the entire process and industrialisation can begin. Stimulated by the desire for greater productivity and better quality, and assured of a growing and interested market, industry will at last be able to move into the twentieth century. The combining of small enterprises into great modern industries, together with a migration of building workers from the open site to the factory building (with all its social advantages), will be an organic outcome of the newly-created situation. With a healthy and mature building industry, we may be just in time to effectively and definitively oppose the wholesale redevelopment of our towns.

The architects

What will be the position of the architect in the new situation we have envisaged? What part will he play in the support-dwelling industry?

In this respect his activities can be separated into three closely-connected spheres: the design of the support structures as constructional system, the design of dwellings to be manufactured by the industry, and the design of the individual dwelling.

It is difficult to foresee in what way the architect will contribute to these three activities. He will obviously be closely associated with the support-dwelling industry, for such an industry will see the importance of using the best designers. The design of support structures and their associated dwelling systems will unquestionably require the attention of specialists. The architect who concerns himself with these problems will have to maintain close contact with the available, possible manufacturing processes, and be in constant touch with the numerous specialists within the industry. On the other hand, he must be able to see the matter as a whole. With the aid of extensive market research he will bring all his talent and inventiveness to bear on designing what is most suitable to the public, and within that framework produce a system which is as variable as possible.

Such a person will probably become something quite different from the current conception of the professional architect. He will, in fact, be more like an industrial designer. He will give the industrial product—the result of a most complex process of factors and influences—its detailed form, in such a way that the public for which it is intended will derive the maximum practical and aesthetic advantages from it.

The industrial designer is himself the product of modern industry, and has already taken his place in the world of production as a sort of bridge between manufacturer and consumer. It is logical, therefore, that he would take up his own valuable position in an industrialised building industry.

All this gives rise to an interesting reflection concerning the role of the architect in future society. It shows that the introduction of the support industry will integrate the architect in an all-embracing process. This need not surprise us, for support structures mean nothing else but the integration of forces, which in MH had lost their mutual balance.

But it also indicates that the architect, as free artist and independent form-giver, will assume a certain anonymity, and will become part of a larger whole. He will no longer be so recognisable in the expression of his housing products, and housing quarters will no longer be a matter for traditional aesthetic preoccupation. In this sphere, the architect will lose his independent artistic personality, in the sense in which he himself likes to see it. If as a result a kind of housing comes about which will give us good and serviceable dwellings, bring back the occupants into the housing process and permit the creation of fine industrial products in accord with society and their time, there will be no reason to mourn.

If this situation should arise, it would also influence architecture outside housing and the architect as artist, as creator of the unique and independent architectural object. This influence is too interesting to bypass altogether, for in considering it, however cursorily, we may form a better idea of the role of the architect and the architectural project in society.

Let us look at the architect in the way he likes to see himself: the artist, the poet in stone, steel and glass; and also look at the building which is his product as a work of art, as materialised poetry. Let us agree that civilisation needs this poetry; indeed that a civilisation can in part be seen as such because of its existence. What then is the organic connection between this special work and the normal everyday buildings which have so far concerned us? Poetry cannot arise without a powerful, living, spontaneously developing language of communication. The poet whose work exceeds the language of everyday conversation is nevertheless in great need of it. The language he hears around him is the source from which he draws. It enriches his work with new images and colours and he gives back what he took from everyday life.

From an architectural point of view, the situation which developed through MH may be seen as a loss of the everyday: the conversation of laymen dried up, and only the poets' dialogue remained—hence the aesthetic character of MH. The architect-poet finds himself in a terrible situation. In his perambulation through the town, he finds that the daily chatter has ceased. He hears only his own verses and those of his colleagues being recited. They are spoken by uniform choirs. Every sound he utters is answered only by the lines of his confreres.

Is it any wonder that sterility threatens and that, cut off from the source which feeds him, he is in danger of losing himself in empty jargon? Looking around for a foothold, the architect grabs at the only thing he can work with—material —and inclines to exaggerated expression. Is it any wonder that, in looking for inspiration and lacking normal criteria, he will search for ever-new forms? He is not motivated by a society of which he is part and he is in need of ideas. These ideas will gradually make him repeat himself. The poet who no longer hears everyday conversation will exhaust himself in increasingly artificial syntax. He will call forth every sound he can think of, for he hears no echo.

To ensure the architecture of the future we should not concern ourselves so much with architecture, as with the building of society, with—at least in housing—simple proficiency without pretensions. When proficiency is rooted deeply in the ordinary world and arises where money, equipment and skills are present for research and development, we shall have a proper foundation for a new architecture. A society which cares about these things and is aware of its ability to make judgments and take note of these developments will also bring about this foundation. Talent capable of producing great achievements will emerge from this background and genius will develop and unfold its full powers, not to the detriment of society, but to show it its true form.

The industrialisation of housing on the support system will mean the end of the architect who wants to live out his artistry by manipulating men and materials, but at the same time it will provide a basis for an architecture rooted in society.

CONCLUSION

The time has come to wind up. There are still problems left to solve, but we have reached a point from which we can take a general view of the new arrangement of forces. The new landscape we survey is still shrouded in mist, but clear orientation points can be discerned. Support structures make a new orientation possible.

> They enable the occupants to be involved via the independent dwelling.
>
> They distinguish between industrial production and site labour.
>
> They distinguish between the general and the particular, thus allowing industrial development to take place, but at the same time they gather both together by an all-embracing industrial apparatus.
>
> They make possible the living, evolving town.
>
> They offer, as the framework of a town, great opportunities in town planning terms.
>
> They bring to an end artificial aspects of the way in which society is housed.
>
> They distinguish between the field of the architect and that of the town planner.
>
> They encourage the growth of a new society.

The idea of support structures and support towns is the idea of a world based upon the realities of human relationships. *No thoughts directed towards a better future can be fruitful unless they couple confidence in human nature with a full exploitation of all useful means.*

If in housing we wish to restore human relationships, but mean to exclude today's technical possibilities, we are following a road to the past, a road we cannot follow. If we wish only to develop the technological potential without touching human relationships, we end up with something like MH. Support towns are to some extent inherent in today's activities. Technology has developed to such a point that a serious study of the notion of support structures is feasible. The impoverishment of human society in MH towns is becoming generally recognised. Like a caterpillar in a cocoon, we have surrounded ourselves with a technical potential which, as yet, has not found its proper purpose. The time has come to free ourselves and regain the initiative.

The continuing development of the present situation will inevitably lead to some kind of support-structure system. There is no question of invention here, but rather of a certain insight. That is why it is necessary to discuss it. We must not allow new forms to overcome us in the way MH came upon us like a natural disaster. Our task is to try and understand what we are doing as clearly as possible, and not to explain and interpret it only after it is done. We must see what the future holds so that we may judge it, come to terms with it, or fight it.

If new forms of human housing offer new opportunities, we must be able to say why they are preferable to old ones. To do that a clear insight is needed into what dwelling really means. Once we agree that it is necessary to introduce the inhabitant or active force into the housing process, we can face the future with confidence. Building has always been a matter of confidence and to make this a reality we must be clear and unequivocal about the nature of man's housing needs.

POSTSCRIPT 1971

What steps can we take to ensure that the natural relationship once again takes its place in the housing process? What experience have we gained since this book was first published? It is now difficult to imagine the situation ten years ago, when problems were of a quantitative nature. The main consideration was the number of dwellings to be produced and housing was in the first place a technical and financial problem. The quality of the living environment was hardly a factor to be considered. Only a few were concerned with it and there was no question of public participation at all. There was a firm faith in building systems and prefabrication: systems and prefabrication, that is, in the context of MH.

Public participation has now become a fashionable term in Holland, and it is all to the good that the self-assurance of specialists and the bureaucratic machine is no longer accepted without question. The users make it clear that they want to be heard. But this does not mean that the need for the restoration of the natural relationship is generally understood, for a public dialogue can very well be carried on in terms of MH. It only means that the voice of the user will be heard in MH. But who speaks for him? Who puts himself forward as his representative? The occupants themselves are as anonymous as before: they remain the passive, unknown consumers of ready-made 'dwellings' turned out by the MH apparatus.

Reintroduction of the natural relationship demands that the specialist will no longer produce ready-made dwellings. It determines what decisions are proper to the individual, and that, if no such decisions are taken, no dwellings will result. It means that lawyers, clients, economists, architects, contractors and all those who play a part in the provision of housing will have to adopt a different way of thinking and working. These roles must be revised. This will not happen at once, but can only result from a slow process, dependent not on technical innovations but on the growth of new insights. Only from this new vision can technical solutions emerge which will factually change the process. The production of support structures and their detachable units is, after all, not a technical problem.

It is therefore not so surprising that in Holland the initiative came from architects. They provided the money, through the setting up of the SAR (Foundation for Architectural Research), to inquire into measures which could enable the industrial apparatus to produce support structures and their detachable units. Architects by no means occupy a position of power in the housing process. On the contrary, in the MH system, they may well become marginal figures. Yet it is they who stand closest to the relationship between man and the built environment. They are trained to make the connections between human problems and technical solutions.

Perhaps the first condition necessary for change in the housing process is that a group of individuals who play a part in it will decide to take action within the framework of the given social context and existing technical possibilities, and insert question marks in the accepted dogmas. The first essential is that work will begin *where one is* in that section of society of which one forms part. We need not wait for circumstances to change before anything can be done. Something has to be done to change the circumstances. In short, there is no other way than 'engagement'.

The second condition is obviously that this engagement must be organised: that is to say, that it will manifest itself in action over a long period. The action of SAR has, in the first place, directed itself towards the role of the architect. Research has been done into the problem of what the designer must do to make support structures and their detachable units possible. After all, one party has to design and produce support structures in the reasonable certainty that decisions will be made in them by, as yet, an unknown occupier, whilst the occupier will have to make use of detachable units designed and produced by another party. Similarly, the industrialist must be reasonably certain that such products can be used in each support structure.

This assumes a system of agreements according to which designers can operate. It requires, in fact, a design method. These agreements therefore had to be developed and they are concerned on the one hand with measurement and on the other with value judgments. In designing a support structure, how can one be sure that this structure is the best possible for the given circumstances? The problem which was thus touched upon led to the consideration of the design process as a decision process. If two parties separately set out to take decisions about products which presently are to be combined by a third party, that is, the occupier, how do they decide what decisions must be made, and how can they do this in such a way that the other parties are aware of the possibilities open to them?

The development of a design method directed towards the realisation of support structures and their elements provided an opportunity to answer many questions. Is it possible to design support structures within the limits set by regulations controlling subsidised housing? Is it possible to design support structures by means of the production systems at present used in housing? Is it possible to make a gradual start? Is it possible at this moment to determine what first steps are best taken? This created confidence and above all the realisation that a step-by-step start can be made, and that a strategy may be set up which slowly but surely will lead to change.

This confidence is also growing because the development of MH itself is becoming increasingly purposeless. There are still not enough dwellings. Production costs are rising at a disturbing rate and they cannot be countered by serial production because opposition to uniformity is increasing more and more. The building organiser constantly has to offer more variety, while at the same time he must produce more efficiently. The investor sees his investment becoming obsolete as a result of changes in living standards and new technical developments and he cannot adapt his dwellings as the years go by. The realisation is dawning that we cannot determine a dwelling which will be viable fifty years hence. In short, MH no longer provides an answer and an alternative must be found. Support structures are not for the year 2000, but for today. Besides, what we build now will be used in the year 2000: we are building towns for the new age today.

The idea that a new vision, presented as a way of designing and acting, can provide answers to the problems of today, has led to serious participation on the part of a few individuals from other disciplines: an investor who wants to take the initiative; contractors wishing to investigate the production of fairly flexible systems; groups working on pilot schemes; an industry which decides to market a set of detachable units; architects' practices which master the methodology and wish to develop it and a great increase in the number of architects supporting the SAR (Foundation for Architectural Research).

As confidence in supports grows, so grows the understanding

that the problems are not mainly of a technical nature. The technical and economic advantages are becoming clear. Serial production and standardisation can at last be seen as means of increasing efficiency without resulting in petrification and uniformity. But the whole machinery of actions, decisions, responsibilities, conventions, regulations and laws is still directed towards MH and all thought processes are based on it. We have hardly begun.

What was originally seen in Holland as a utopia is now beginning to be accepted as a serious alternative. It is true that the number of people from various disciplines working in this direction is relatively small, and that there are no large scale proposals, nor finances for broadly based undertakings. But things are happening under the difficult conditions of everyday practice, and though this is by no means spectacular, it may be more important.

Building and living are activities which more than any other are tied to geographical and social situations. But the natural relationship between man and his dwelling is universal. Wherever towns are growing, where population problems are increasing, and the development of production technique is going on, wherever social patterns are changing and the traditional forms of housing no longer apply, there the natural relationship must come into play. The solution must be found according to time and place, but the problem is the same.